TIME AFTER TYME

KAY DIBIANCA

Wordstar Publishing

Time After Tyme / DiBianca —1st ed.

10 9 8 7 6 5 4 3 2 1

Cover design by Kristie Koontz.

For my cousin Joan

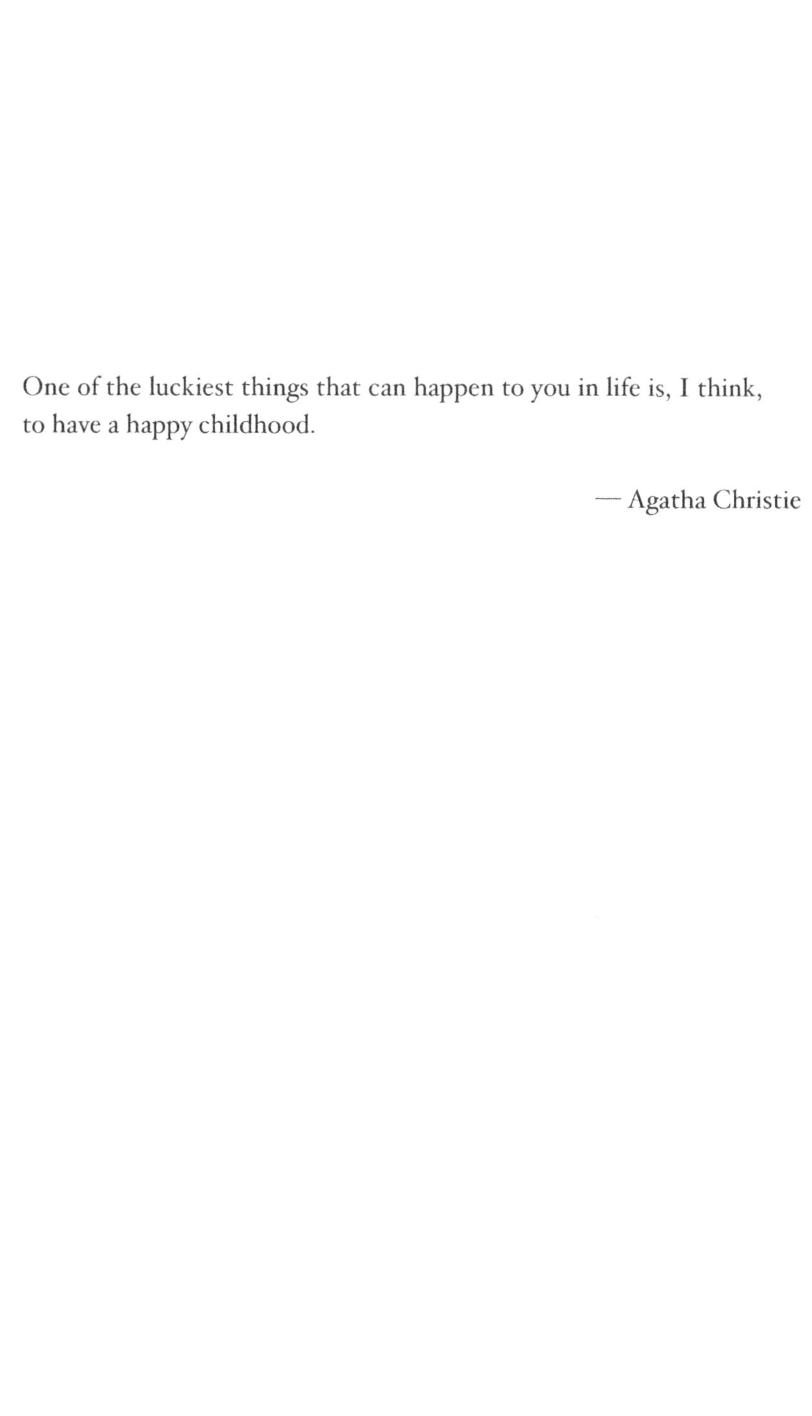

One of the luckiest things that can happen to you in life is, I think, to have a happy childhood.

— Agatha Christie

ACKNOWLEDGMENTS

I am deeply grateful to the people who have made this book possible through their generous guidance, counsel, love, and ideas.

I am fortunate to have worked with exceptional editors in the process of creating and finalizing the story. My developmental editor, Mel Hughes, provided her professional expertise in story-telling to help me keep the action moving. Barbara Curtis supplied her meticulous line-editing talents and thoughtful feedback, and I had the good fortune to work with the talented Jodie Renner as she proofread and edited the final draft. Their experience and commitment to excellence has made this a much better book

I am also in debt to the folks who helped me with various aspects of the story. These include Division Chief Todd Grant of the Memphis Fire Department, Fire Marshal Jody Dwyer of the Germantown Fire Department, Curtis Keech, Tim Cartwright, and Barbara Radinsky.

I am very thankful to my wonderful friends and colleagues who read the entire manuscript and recommended improvements, many of which are included in the final version: Jan and Gary Keyes, Debbie Burke, Steve Hooley, Larry and Julia Siler, Angela Mutzi, and Lisa Simonds.

And I owe a special debt of gratitude to James Scott Bell whose books, courses, and blog posts on the craft of writing have inspired and edified me throughout my writing journey.

Finally, I thank my wonderful husband, Frank, a fellow novelist who provided numerous ideas for the book, and whose joyful approach to living inspires me every day.

"The LORD is my strength and my shield; in him my heart trusts, and I am helped; my heart exults, and with my song I give thanks to him." — Psalm 28:7

Chapter One

REEN OUT ON A LIMB

The branch made a creaky noise when I crawled out on it, and the ground looked really far away. I wasn't worried, though. Oak tree limbs don't break.

"Psst." My cousin Joanie tried to whisper, but it sounded more like a moose wheezing. Joanie is nine years old, but she never learned how to whisper properly. She was sitting on a low branch like she was glued to the trunk of the tree.

A squirrel poked his head out of a knothole and gnawed on an acorn while he stared at me. Like he was surprised to see a girl halfway out on a limb. But this is my life. An investigative reporter knows no fear.

"Psst, Reen. Stop." Joanie's voice got louder and scaredier as I inched my way along the branch.

"Shh." I whispered back with much better form. "I want to hear what they're saying."

It's good practice for a reporter to eavesdrop on possible subjects, and I'd radared in on Phil Warren as he walked across campus with his girlfriend. They were so wrapped up in each other, they didn't even see us. They stopped next to a big elm tree a few feet away, and the girl stood with her back against the trunk while he leaned toward her with his hand on the tree and a goofy expression on his face.

I'll never understand adults. If Phil was trying to impress his girlfriend, he'd do better if he stood on his head or did a couple of cartwheels. At least it would show a little talent. Maybe he could buy a yo-yo.

I crept another couple of inches forward, eased the notebook out of my pocket, and strained to hear. He called the girl Kathryn. I wrote it down.

Kathryn was saying something about Reverend Whitefield. I know him. He's the minister at the university chapel. She said, "He asked me to stop by today after lunch. It's about Mr. Tyme."

Mr. Tyme? Wasn't he the librarian who died in that fire?

Kathryn frowned. "Reverend Whitefield thinks there may have been foul play."

Foul play? Murder! My heart pounded and my future life unfolded in front of me like a YouTube video. I could solve the mystery and expose the killer! I'd be famous. I'd be rich. I'd be one of those people who gets a college degree without having to go to school.

Wait. She was talking again, but her voice was so low, I couldn't hear, so I tried to ease forward, but my foot caught on something. I looked back and saw my shoelace tangled around a twig. I tugged, but it wouldn't come loose.

Joanie and the squirrel were both staring at me with their mouths hanging open. I pulled again, but it wouldn't give. I tried to stretch myself like Elastigirl. No go. That twig was going to make me miss the most important news story of my life.

In situations like this, a reporter should ditch the finesse and go for brute strength, so I gritted my teeth and yanked my leg as hard as I could. The twig broke, my foot flew up in the air, and I fell backward.

The tree made a huge popping sound, and leaves spun around me like a green tornado. Joanie screamed, "Reeeen!" The squirrel dropped his acorn and dove back into the hole in the tree. And the branch fell out from under me.

Not good.

Chapter Two

DROPPING INTO A MYSTERY

CRACK!

The powerful crash of a tree limb breaking reverberated across the quad and made Kathryn jump. She grabbed Phil's arm, and together they stared in horror as a branch of the oak tree hit the ground with a young girl wrapped around it.

They rushed to the child's side, expecting blood and tears, but instead, the girl untangled herself from the bark and jumped up.

"Are you all right?" Kate asked.

"Yes. I'm fine." The little face wore a nonchalant expression, as if falling out of trees was a daily occurrence of no particular importance. She looked to be about ten years old, with plain features, short brown hair, and blue-gray eyes. When she smiled, she displayed teeth that seemed to want a little more room to maneuver than there was available in her mouth. She wore blue coveralls over a white T-shirt.

"What were you doing in that tree?" Kate asked.

The girl's countenance lifted. "I'm an investigative reporter," she said, "and I keep an eye on what's going on around campus."

Phil leaned forward. "You should know better than to climb out on an old rotten limb like that, Reen. You could have hurt yourself."

"You know her?" Kate turned toward Phil.

"Yes," he said. "Kathryn Frasier, meet Irene Penterson."

"People call me Reen," the child said. "Rhymes with keen."

Phil's expression changed to an almost-smile. "Her father is a customer of mine. She comes with him when he brings his car in. Reen likes to talk to the people waiting for their cars. She says she's investigating our operation." He picked up the notebook Reen had dropped and glanced at it. "Were you eavesdropping on us?"

Reen's expression went blank.

Phil crossed his arms over his chest. "That means were you listening to what we were saying."

"I know what it means. But an investigative reporter doesn't eavesdrop. We investigate." She brushed at her overalls. "And we never reveal our methods."

Phil sighed and handed her the notebook.

A second child appeared at the base of the tree. This one was a sweet-looking girl, complete with bright red hair pulled back in two ponytails, freckles spreading out over a button nose, and green eyes that were demurely looking up at Kate. She wore a green polka-dot top over black leggings. All her features seemed to be in the right places, and there wasn't a smudge in sight. A tiny rosebud mouth stammered, "R-Reen, are you okay?"

"Yes, Joanie, I'm okay," the other one retorted and tossed her head.

Kate gestured toward the little redhead. "And who is this?"

"That's my cousin Joanie. She's my assistant." Reen leaned toward Kate and said under her breath. "Joanie's too young to be a real assistant. She's only nine."

Joanie blushed until her ears glowed and the freckles stood out like tiny purple periods across her nose and cheeks.

"And how old are you?" Kate asked.

"I'm eleven." Reen lifted her chin in triumph and wiped a hand across her mouth.

"You're not eleven," Joanie said. "You're only ten."

Reen scowled. "Well, I'll be eleven soon."

Kate touched her elbow. "You've scraped your arm. We should take you to the infirmary."

"No, I'm fine. My father says I'm the active type."

"And so he does." A thin man with blazing red hair and rimless glasses strode toward them. He wore a white dress shirt and gray slacks, and he leaned down to inspect the girl's injury. "Skinned elbows are Reen's specialty," he said and smiled up at Kate. He probed the child's arm around the injury. "Does it hurt?"

"No, Dad."

"Any other scrapes?" He held her chin and turned her head from side to side.

"No."

"Well, that's not too bad for the first day of summer vacation." He tousled her hair. "Maybe you could give the trees a little time off. I'm not sure they're up to a Reen summer yet."

Reen laughed and hugged him. "Okay, Dad."

He stood and offered his hand to Kate. "I'm Nate Penterson, Reen's father." He put his other hand on his daughter's shoulder. "I also serve as elbow repairer, healer of bruised knees, and all-around nursemaid. Reen keeps me so busy, I hardly have time for my regular job." He nodded to Phil. "Phil, what are you doing on campus on a Monday in the middle of the day?"

Phil shook his hand. "I came over to have lunch with my girl," he said. "This is Kathryn Frasier. She has a meeting here later today."

"Well, I'm glad you have such a beautiful day to enjoy each other. You'll have to excuse me, though. I have a meeting to prepare for." He turned back to his daughter. "Reen, you and Joan should go to the house. I'm sure Mrs. Toussaint has lunch for you."

"Yes, sir." Reen smiled innocently, but she didn't move.

Penterson turned to walk away. "Phil, drop by and let's have lunch together one of these days."

"Sure thing. I'll give you a call."

Kate looked at her watch. "I'd better be going. I'm supposed to meet Cece in a few minutes. She's finishing up a rehearsal in the drama department."

Phil took her hand. "You have time to walk me to my car." As they strolled back through the quad, Kate heard little footsteps behind them.

Phil looked back over his shoulder. "Didn't your father tell you to go home and have lunch?" he asked Reen, who was following close behind them with Joanie beside her. Reen shrugged and kept following. He leaned toward Kate and said in a low voice, "I'm going to give her something to write about."

When they got to his car, he grabbed Kate around the waist and said in a loud voice, "Honey, I can't wait until tonight." Then he pulled her in and gave her a long, passionate kiss.

Joanie and Reen both gasped. Phil released Kate, turned to the little girls, and winked. "So long, ladies."

When he drove away, Joanie took Kate's hand and sighed. "That was like a movie kiss."

Reen grabbed her other hand. "Tell us about the murder!"

Chapter Three

LITTLE GIRL HELP

"Murder?" Kathryn said. "What murder?"

Reen stared eagerly at her. "I heard you say there was a murder. We want to help you solve it."

"There's no murder," Kate said. "I'm on my way to meet my sister. She's an actress and she should be finishing rehearsal soon."

She walked toward the bell tower with a young girl hanging on to each of her hands. On her right, Joanie's hand was soft and small, and she took little mincing steps as they made their way through the center of the quad.

On the other side, she could feel the calluses on Reen's hand, and she smiled inwardly, remembering her own adventures falling out of trees as a tomboy.

The campus was almost deserted during the break between spring semester and the beginning of summer session. A few graduate students ambled from one building to another, but the undergrads were gone, and many faculty members took advantage of the lull to travel or vacation with their families.

Joanie pulled at Kate's hand. "Phil looks like a movie star," she said. "He's so handsome."

Kate smiled at the little redhead who was looking up at her in wonder. "Yes, he is, isn't he?"

"What's your sister's name?" Reen asked.

"Her name is Cece. She should be here shortly." They reached the bench under Bellevue University's iconic aspen tree.

"We'll keep an eye out for her," Reen said. "Does she look like you?"

"No." Kate smiled. "She and I are entirely different. You see my hair?" She pulled at her ponytail. "How would you describe it?"

"It's brown," Reen said.

"And it's long and straight," Joanie added.

"Right. But Cece's hair is curly and blonde. Now, what about my eyes?" She removed her sunglasses and opened her eyes wide.

The two girls put their faces close to hers. "Brown!" Joanie shouted out.

"Right again. But Cece's eyes are blue." Kate stood as straight and tall as she could. "Would you say I'm tall or short?"

"Tall!" Reen said.

"Yep. But Cece is petite."

Joanie tilted her head and knitted her ginger-colored brows together. "How can you be sisters if you don't look alike?"

Reen turned to her cousin. "It's all genetics, Joanie. People can inherit different genes even if they have the same parents."

"That's right," Kate said and turned to Joanie. "You and Reen are cousins, but you don't look anything alike."

Reen nodded. "Joanie's mother and my dad are sister and brother. All the Pentersons have red hair and freckles, and Joanie takes after her mom. That's why she looks more like my dad than I do." She brushed her hair back from her face. "I look more like my mom."

"What does your mom do?"

"My mom died," Reen said quietly.

"Oh, honey, I'm so sorry." Kate stooped down to be on the same level as Reen and held her by the arms.

"It's okay," Reen said. "She died a long time ago. I was just a baby. I don't remember her at all." Then she smiled. "But we have pictures of her."

"I bet she was very pretty."

"She was beautiful. And Joanie's mother is pretty, too. Aunt Melissa looks like a big version of Joanie. She works in the personnel office."

"Well, that's very impressive." Kate smiled at the two little ones.

"What's impressive?" A new voice entered the conversation as Cece waltzed up, wearing a pair of round sunglasses with blue lenses. She had on a sleeveless black turtleneck, blue jeans, and fuchsia-colored running shoes. She had hooked her red windbreaker over a finger, and it draped over her right shoulder. Her blonde hair bounced as she approached.

"You must be Cece." Reen said.

"That's right. How did you know?"

"Kathryn told us what you look like, and she said you're an actress." Joanie said.

Cece smiled and dropped into a deep curtsy. "So I am." Then she shook hands with each girl while Kate introduced them.

"Are you ready to go meet with Reverend Whitefield? Do you know what he wants to talk to us about?" Cece asked Kate.

"It's a murder!" Reen blurted out.

"Murder?" Cece's voice hit a high note.

Kathryn shook her head at Reen, then she turned to Cece and pointed to the opposite side of the quad. "Reen was in that old oak tree over there. She was listening in on a conversation I had with Phil, and she must have jumped to the conclusion that Reverend Whitefield wants to talk to us about a murder."

"That's a little melodramatic, isn't it?" Cece asked.

Joanie looked confused. "What's mellow dramatics?"

"It's just a word. Melodramatic means something like over the top. You know, too much to be believed." Cece did a mock salute to Reen. "We'll get the full scoop and report back, Captain."

"We can go with you," Reen said.

"No, Reen." Kate's voice was firm. "Your father wanted you to go home and have lunch." She tweaked the child's ear. "We'll take it from here."

Reen frowned. Joanie giggled and looked shyly up at Cece. "I want to be an actress."

"You do?" Cece smiled down at her. "Good for you. Maybe you can come watch a rehearsal for the play I'm in. We'll be doing dress rehearsals soon, and you can see all the actors in their costumes."

"Oh, goodie." Joanie jumped up and down and clapped her hands. "Reen, we can go watch a play!"

Reen grunted. "I don't care about a stupid play. I want to find the murderer."

"I think you need to find something else to be interested in," Kate said.

As she spoke, the bell in the clock tower chimed once.

"I know what we can do," Cece said. "One day soon, we'll take you on a tour of the bell tower and look at the mechanism for the clock. I'll explain how a clock works."

"You know about clocks?" Joanie's eyes were wide with wonder.

Cece nodded. "Yep. I used to repair watches at my father's jewelry store, and I can show you all about how the clock in the bell tower keeps time. It'll be fun."

"I'd like that," Reen said. She traded her frown for a smile and spoke the words as she wrote in her notebook. "Cece will teach us how a clock works." She looked back up. "When?"

"How about tomorrow? I have rehearsals in the morning, but we can meet at one-thirty and then we can be in the tower when the clock strikes two and the gong sounds."

Reen put her notebook back in her pocket and took a cell phone out of another pocket. She punched at it a few times and looked up. "One-thirty tomorrow. Got it."

Cece gave them both a big smile. "We'll use the experience to learn about time."

"Wow. That's amazing," Reen said.

"What?"

"The man who was murdered. His name was Tyme!"

Chapter Four

MR. VENERO

Kate waved to the two young girls as they walked away, then turned to her sister. "This certainly has been an unusual morning."

"You seem to have a gift for getting involved in unusual things," Cece said with a smirk.

Kate motioned for Cece to follow as she headed toward the rectory. "Yeah, I know. It's my special talent."

Cece trotted to catch up. "How did Reen get the idea of a murder?"

"She heard me say Reverend Whitefield mentioned the possibility of foul play in Mr. Tyme's death, and she jumped to the conclusion it was murder."

"That's usually what foul play means, isn't it?" Cece asked. "I would probably have come to the same conclusion." She looked up at her sister. "What do you know about Mr. Tyme?"

"Not much. He was the university librarian and he died in a fire. I guess we'll soon find out what this is all about."

They approached the house that stood in the shade of a group of white birches just south of the chapel. A sidewalk led to the front door of the home and a gardener was kneeling and working on flowering plants at the edge of the walkway. He wore a wide-brim hat and was carefully placing a green sprout into the ground.

"Those flowers are beautiful," Cece said and stopped to admire them. "What are they?"

The gardener jerked his head around, apparently startled by the sudden intrusion. He stood and looked at Cece in awkward silence for a few seconds.

His face was tanned and weathered under a floppy, big-brim hat. When he pulled his gloves off, Kate noticed his long, tapered fingers.

"They're impatiens," he said in a hoarse, whispery voice, "and those over there are silver artemisias." He gestured toward the side of the house.

"They're absolutely lovely," Kate said. "Are those honeysuckle bushes by the fence?"

He turned his head to see where she was pointing. "Yes."

He took a pocket watch out of his pants pocket, and Kate saw a vein throbbing on the side of his temple as he opened the watch and stared at the time. Then he replaced the watch, dropped back to his knees, and pulled the trowel out of the dirt.

"Smells wonderful," she said, but he didn't respond.

Jan Whitefield, petite and sturdy, bounded out from the front door. She had on blue jeans, a green T-shirt with "Shalom!" written on the front, and New Balance running shoes. "Hello there." She beamed and gave each of the young women a firm hug. "I see you've met Mr. Venero. He's the genius who keeps the grounds around the rectory looking like a proper English garden."

An unsmiling Venero nodded to her and then turned back to his work.

Kate smiled down at the minister's wife. "Reverend Whitefield asked us to stop by," she said. "Something about Mr. Tyme."

"Yes, I know," Jan said. "Come in. We'll wait for Jim inside."

* * *

Zachary Venero glanced over his shoulder as the women walked away. He wiped his face with a handkerchief and rubbed at the sweat on the back of his neck.

The visitors had made him feel uncomfortable. Strangers always did. They were like new pieces of a puzzle that didn't fit.

He dug a fresh hole and retrieved a little plant from the tray. Planting was a gift from God. He didn't have to think beyond the flower bed. Every little root and bulb had its place in God's creation, and his job was to keep it orderly.

He looked at the front of the rectory and wondered about the three women on the other side of the door. He had heard the tall one say something about Mr. Tyme. Why were they talking about him? Mr. Tyme had been a nice man. Sometimes he had stopped to talk and even showed him the puzzles he was working on. He liked to figure things out. He said Zack was a natural at solving problems.

He closed his eyes and tried to concentrate, but he was beginning to feel the pressure inside his head again. What had his father told him? "Don't concern yourself with other people's business. Concentrate on your job. Working the soil is a wonderful way to be close to God."

He opened his eyes and looked at the seedling in his hands. He gently untangled the roots, placed it in the hole, and arranged the dirt around it. He brushed a fleck of gravel off one of the petals and stood to admire his work. The semi-circle of pink and white impatiens outlined the space around the delicate white birch tree.

The thin limbs of the tree seemed to lean down and protect the tiny flowers from the summer sun. But the impatiens would only last through the season, then they would die. He bowed his head and murmured, "The grass withers, the flower fades, but the word of our God will stand forever." Life and death. He put his hand in his pants pocket and felt the cool, silver case of the pocket watch.

Chapter Five

REEN HAS LUNCH

"Irene Elizabeth Penterson!" Mrs. Toussaint always uses my full name when she wants to pile on the guilt. The bigger the sin, the more syllables she adds. She calls me "Irene" for small infractions like not finishing my lunch. "Irene Elizabeth" is for mid-sized sins like bossing Joanie around. Today it looked like she hit the jackpot. Guilty in nine syllables.

She pasted the Band-Aid on my arm. "You *must* be more careful. You're going to have scars up and down your body if you keep climbing every tree in sight. You'll be sorry when you become a young lady. Nobody will want to marry you."

Mrs. Toussaint lives in the guesthouse behind our home. She's sort of like a substitute mother, and I think she wants to be sure to fill me up with all the stuff a mother is supposed to care about. She's big on manners, and being a proper lady is super important to her. She's always talking about how you have to eat with the right fork and all that. My father says at least I'm learning how to set the table.

Mrs. Toussaint used to be a first-grade teacher. I bet she was pretty scary to the little kids because she's tall and skinny and her nose is long and pointy and her eyebrows jump up and down when she gets irritated. Also, she wears her dark hair pulled straight back in a tight bun. That's always scary.

She treats me like I'm one of her students and says I need to behave like the intelligent person I am. She even shook her finger at me one day when I told her I'd eaten my whole sandwich, but she found the crust in the potted plant next to my chair. She told me lying was a terrible sin and I should be ashamed. That was a nine-syllable day. She didn't even give me a cookie.

Sometimes I think her idea of a young lady is somebody who wears a frilly dress and high heels and sits around waiting for Mr. Perfect to show up. I'll never be that person. I'm going to be like Amelia Earhart. She was a tomboy, too. She wore pants and flew airplanes. Maybe I'll take flying lessons when I'm old enough.

Mrs. Toussaint likes to talk about balance in life. Sometimes she gets so carried away telling me about how you have to be humble and good that she spreads too much pimento cheese on the bread and my sandwich gets all squishy. Today is one of those days. Joanie was lucky because she brought a tomato and avocado wrap her mother made for her.

Mrs. Toussaint had flopped two pieces of bread on the sideboard and was taking the lid off the tub of pimento cheese when I asked her about Mr. Tyme. She goes to church a lot, so she probably knew him.

"Mr. Tyme? Who told you about him?" She stopped digging in the cheese spread and looked at me.

"I heard some people talking about him today. They said he died in a fire. Did you know him?"

She hesitated, and I was afraid she was going to brush me off the way adults do when they decide you're out of order. But she didn't. Her face got kind of soft looking, and she leaned against the countertop. "Yes, I knew him. He was a very nice man."

"How did he die?"

She made a little clicking noise with her tongue and turned her back to me. I had to lean forward to hear her. "There was a fire in his office at the university library. Such a tragedy to happen to that good man." She turned back around to look at me and had an expression like *conversation over*. She pointed the knife at me. "Drink your milk."

What is it with adults? They think they can deter you from your course just by changing the subject. No way is this investigative reporter going to fall for that. "Did you ever go to the university library?"

"No." She dipped more pimento cheese out of the tub. "I always used the library at our school. I have no need for all the fancy works they have in the university library." She was becoming a one-woman pimento cheese machine.

"I go to the university library sometimes."

She stopped and looked at me again. "Why on earth would you go there? You have a whole room full of books."

I decided not to talk about Mr. Tyme and the library anymore when I saw what she was doing to my sandwich.

"Here." She finally plunked the dish down in front of me.

It was a monster-size sandwich. Pimento-saurus Rex.

* * *

Doris Toussaint stood at the back door and watched the two youngsters as they walked away from the house. She had made them go to Reen's room to rest for a few minutes after lunch and had explained how important it is to let your food digest before being active. Joanie had put her dishes in the sink and skipped off to count how many dresses Reen had in her closet. Reen had grumbled that she had too much work to do, but she trudged back to her room all the same.

How much did Reen really know about Mr. Tyme? Could she know that Mr. Tyme was an occasional visitor at Doris's home? Surely two little girls couldn't get the police involved again. It had been so easy when they interviewed her about Mr. Tyme shortly after the fire. The police only wanted to know when she had last seen him and if he had said anything unusual. She had lied, of course, but it was just a small one. There was no need for the Bellevue police to know that he was more to her than a colleague.

They had kept their relationship quiet. He had wanted that more than she. He had insisted on it, as a matter of fact, fearing that having a romantic relationship with a divorced woman would make a bad name for him in the church. He was a deacon, after all.

She sank down in one of the kitchen chairs. Clarence Tyme. He had been such a considerate, attentive friend. Of course, people would talk if they knew he came to visit her in her home every Friday night, but they had been very discreet. No one could possibly know.

She recalled the last visit he had visited her. He had seemed distracted, jiggling his keys and jabbering on about some kind of strange notes he had seen. She had begun to think he was looking for an excuse to break off their relationship. After all they had shared, how could he?

But if the children stirred up trouble, the police might come back asking questions. Maybe she should go visit her sister in Duluth. No. They'd just get in touch with her there. She'd have to wait and watch. Reen was an impossible child, but maybe she could get her interested in something else. Yes. That was it. Come up with something new for Reen so she would drop this silly obsession with being a reporter.

Chapter Six

REVEREND WHITEFIELD'S DILEMMA

The familiar aroma of warm scones brought an immediate sense of comfort and security to Kate as they stepped into the living room of the rectory. She had sat in this room many times for Bible studies, youth group meetings, and, within the last year, for counseling after her parents' untimely deaths.

The worn couch and chairs bore witness to the fact that the owners of this home cared more about the people who visited than the furniture they sat on. Wall hangings with scriptural references offered comfort to the disheartened. Large windows provided a sunny view of the garden. It was a room full of encouragement and hope, though sadly, no pictures of children.

"Have a seat," Jan said as she bobbed toward the kitchen. "Jim is over at the chapel meeting with one of our church committees, but he'll be back in a minute. I'll just get a little snack for us." She returned with a tray of teacups and blueberry scones. "Here we are." She put the tray on the coffee table and poured tea for each of the girls.

Cece sipped from the china teacup. "The flowers around your house really are magnificent. Mr. Venero must be an extremely talented man."

"Yes, he is. The university is fortunate to have him." Jan passed the plate of scones to each of the women.

"He seems a little ... unusual," Cece said. "I don't think he was comfortable with us."

"Zack lives in his own world," Jan replied. "It would be wrong to force him into ours." She put her teacup down. "It's rather a sad story—" Before she could finish, the front door opened, and Reverend Whitefield's tall, lanky frame filled the entryway. As a young child, Kate had been in awe of this quiet giant with his kind demeanor. Lately, his once-erect posture had softened, and his shoulders stooped a bit.

"Kathryn and Cece, thank you for coming over." His mouth formed a smile, but his clear brown eyes, which usually radiated the joy of the gospel, were dim. Kate stiffened, wondering what could make the amiable minister look so concerned. Did something happen at his committee meeting? He leaned down and gave his wife a peck on the cheek.

"Do you want a cup of tea, Jim?" his wife asked.

"No, thanks," he said and motioned them toward the back of the rectory. "I'd like you all to come back to my study. There's something I want you to see."

As they walked down the long hall, Jan said, "Can you give us a hint what this is about, Jim?"

The reverend stopped with his hand on the door to the study and turned to face them. "I think it may have to do with a murder."

* * *

"Murder?" Kate said. They all entered the reverend's study, and he closed the door behind them.

Overflowing bookcases lined the walls, and a desk in the middle of the room housed stacks of papers and several Bibles. There were four straight-back chairs in front of the desk and a credenza against the wall under the lone window. With the shades drawn, it had the feeling of a scholarly retreat used for serious study and reflection.

"I'm afraid it may be so." Reverend Whitefield gestured for them to take a seat. He walked around the desk, settled into his own chair, and leaned forward with his arms on the desk. "Kathryn, did you know Mr. Tyme?"

"I remember him. He was the head librarian at the university library."

"Mr. Tyme was also a deacon in the chapel." Reverend Whitefield sighed. "He was a good friend and highly regarded on campus. Many people referred to him affectionately as Father Time."

"Father Time?" Cece said.

The minister chuckled gently. "That's an epithet given to him by some of the faculty members here at the university. You see, Mr. Tyme had a lot of interests, and one of them, for obvious reasons, was the subject of time. Along with all his other activities, he maintained the clock in the university bell tower. Some years ago, the label got pasted to him and it stuck."

"How did he die?" Cece asked.

Reverend Whitefield took a deep breath and interlaced his fingers. "As you may have heard, Mr. Tyme died in a fire at the library. His death was determined to have been an accident."

"But you think it was murder?" Kate asked.

The minister ran a hand through his full head of straight white hair. "I'm not sure, but something happened recently that has me worried, so I wanted to talk to you. I know your powers of analysis, Kathryn, and I know you can keep a confidence, so I'd like to get your opinion."

"I don't know if I can be of any help, but I'll try."

"Here's the sequence of events the night of the fire, at least the way I understand it. Mr. Tyme had closed the library and locked it after everyone else had left. That was his usual routine. Then he went to his office in the basement of the building. That room also contained a lot of books and papers. There was a fire in the room and Mr. Tyme died of smoke inhalation."

"Why do you think it was suspicious?"

"The medical examiner found a wound on the back of his head. The police theorize he tripped over something in the office, hit his head on a sharp bookend that was on the edge of his desk, and was knocked unconscious. A cigarette he was smoking ignited the papers. He was a heavy smoker, you see. With all the papers and books, the room went up in flames immediately."

"I'm surprised he was smoking down there," Kate said. "It's against the rules to smoke in the library."

The reverend frowned. "I thought the same thing. The assistant librarian, Miss Culberson, said Mr. Tyme always went to the smoking area outside the back door of the library to have a cigarette. But she couldn't be sure he didn't occasionally sneak a smoke when he was in his office. The police found an ashtray there."

"It's a good thing the whole library didn't go up in flames," Cece said.

Whitefield nodded. "Fortunately, the room had been built with extra fortification because the library board thought they might eventually want to use it to store rare books and journals. The fire was confined mostly to the office, but once the smoke got into the corridor, it set off fire alarms, and the Bellevue Fire Department was able to limit it to the basement area."

"If Mr. Tyme had already locked the library, then a murderer would have to have been inside already," Kate said.

Reverend Whitefield's face turned dark. "I fear Mr. Tyme had set up a meeting with someone in his office and that person killed him."

"But if the library was locked when the fire fighters arrived, how would the killer have gotten out of the building?" Cece asked.

"I'm not sure, but that's why I wanted to talk to the two of you. There are a lot of unanswered questions."

"If you think it could have been murder, why not talk to the police?" Kate asked.

"I did talk to the police a week ago, but they think the original police report is correct, and they don't think my new evidence is important."

"New evidence?" Kate asked.

"I'll show you, but first, I need to give you a little history about the prayer box."

Chapter Seven

THE PRAYER BOX

"What's the prayer box?" Cece asked.

Reverend Whitefield pointed toward the university chapel. "We have a box in the foyer of the chapel. It has a small slit in the top and it's locked, so people can drop in their prayer requests with the assurance that their request will be kept confidential."

Kate pulled on her ponytail. "I remember the prayer box. I've used it before."

"One of Mr. Tyme's responsibilities as a deacon was to bring the slips of paper from the prayer box to my office after Sunday services so we could pray over them. After we prayed over them, he would burn them to ensure they remained confidential."

"Sounds like a wonderful system," Cece said.

"We sometimes get things that aren't really prayer requests. You know, children will occasionally put something foolish in the prayer box like 'Please pray that my teacher will give us all A's, so I won't have to do homework anymore.' Sometimes the handwriting is hard to read or there may be other issues, but it's a good system, and the people who submit sincere requests are comforted to know others are praying for them."

"Do you always pray over each one?" Cece asked.

"Yes. Even when we're not sure about the meaning, we lift the person up to the Lord in prayer."

"Last winter, we got an unusual slip of paper. I remember the time of year because Mr. Tyme made a comment about God remembering us at Christmas time." He shrugged. "My memory isn't what it used to be. I don't remember exactly what the note said, but it was typed, and it had an unusual message at the top. Mr. Tyme thought it might be some kind of code, but we couldn't make any sense out of it." He looked up at them. "The bottom of the note said 'God Remembers.'"

"Did you say any kind of prayer for it?"

"Oh, yes. Since it wasn't signed, we offered up a general prayer for the anonymous writer."

"Did Mr. Tyme burn that one?" Kate asked.

"I assume he did. It was his job to burn all the requests. Then a couple of months later, we got another one that was unsigned. I vaguely remember there was a strange, typed line at the top, and again the bottom line said 'God Remembers.' It was obviously related in some way to the first one. We didn't understand the meaning of it, but we prayed over that one as well. I got busy with other things and forgot about it."

"But you think Mr. Tyme discovered something?" Kate asked.

"The day before he died, I was out of town for a conference. I had called him to see how things were going, and he told me he had found out something about those prayer requests. He thought they had some bearing on events that had happened at the university. He was very anxious to tell me about it but didn't want to talk over the phone. He said he had set up a meeting with someone and would tell me the outcome when I returned to Bellevue."

"He didn't tell you who he was meeting with?" Cece asked.

"No. The only other thing I remember is that he said he had something on his plate."

"What does that mean?" Kate asked.

"I'm not sure. It was noisy at the conference, and I may have misunderstood." He sighed. "That was the last time I talked to him."

"You think he met someone who killed him and set the room on fire to cover their crimes?"

Reverend Whitefield sat back in his chair. "I didn't think that at first. I thought it was an accident like the police report said." He opened his desk drawer and pulled out a slip of paper. "A couple of weeks ago, I found this in the prayer box." He handed the paper to Kate.

There were four typewritten lines on the note.

```
A TIME TO LIVE AND A TIME TO DIE
YOU WILL HEAP BURNING COALS ON HIS HEAD
WAPSPAHIODDPSABEMOKIKITIODIL
GOD REMEMBERS
```

Kate read the first line out loud. "A time to live and a time to die." She looked up at the minister. "That's a verse from Ecclesiastes, isn't it?"

"Ecclesiastes 3:2, but it's not exactly the same. The biblical verse in my version actually reads 'a time to be born, and a time to die,'" he said. "Please read the second line."

Kate held the paper in front of her again. "You will heap burning coals on his head."

"That doesn't sound nice," Cece said.

"It's also from the Bible," Jan said. "It's a proverb, right, Jim?"

"It's the first line of Proverbs 25:22." A cloud passed in front of the sun, and the room grew dark as they considered what had been read. "Do you see why I'm suspicious?" Whitefield said. "The first reference talks about a time to die. Even though the spelling of Mr. Tyme's name is different, it's pronounced the same. Then the second Scripture refers to burning coals. That fits with a fire. This one is typed like the other ones. It also has 'God Remembers' written at the bottom. It has to be related to the other requests we received."

"The third line looks like a bunch of random letters. Did you show this to the police?" Kate asked.

"Yes. They examined the paper for fingerprints, but the only ones on it were mine. They thought I was just running down a rabbit hole because I felt bad about Mr. Tyme." He shook his head. "Maybe they're right. Maybe this was left by someone with a terrible sense of humor or maybe it's just a coincidence, but I can't get over this feeling of dread. If the note was left by a murderer, then we may have a killer on the loose in Bellevue. Maybe on this campus." He laid his hand gently on his desk. "I'm convinced this note was written by the same person who wrote the others, but I can't make sense out of it." He shook his head. "I'm not a cryptographer, and I feel helpless."

Kate showed the note to Cece. "Look at the third line. It must be a coded message."

Cece glanced at the paper and handed it back. "If you don't understand it, I'm sure I won't."

Kate turned toward her minister. "What do you want us to do?"

Reverend Whitefield clasped his hands together. "Kathryn, I'm going to ask you to undertake something that could be dangerous. I'm willing to help in any way, but I don't have the expertise in problem-solving that you have. And, frankly, there are few people I trust enough to give this information to. I want you to see if you can decrypt the code on the third line. If you can, we might be able to understand what's going on."

"Of course. I'll give it a try."

"But we have to keep this information confidential. We must be careful. If there is a murderer, we don't want to alert him or her to the fact that we're looking into it." He gestured toward the window that looked out on the university grounds. "And we don't want to start a rumor about a possible murder that could cause a panic on campus."

"I see, but I'll have to tell Phil, and Cece will certainly want to tell Ben." She looked at her sister who nodded vigorously.

"I understand," the minister said. "Just make sure they know this is confidential. We can only share it with others if they absolutely need to know."

Chapter Eight

CHAIRMAN OF THE DEPARTMENT

Nate Penterson made his way past the graduate student labs in the computer science department and into the administration office. He paused next to the admin's desk. "Margaret, how's everything going? Any new disasters I need to know about?"

Margaret Asher looked up at him. She was a big woman with a fleshy face and a wide smile that had welcomed professors and students to the department for over twenty years. Today, however, she wore a decidedly sour expression. "Andrew Bellinger was here a few minutes ago. He seemed quite agitated. Said he wanted to talk to you right away."

Nate sighed. Andrew always wanted to talk right away. "How's my schedule for the rest of the day?"

"You don't have any appointments until meeting the new chancellor at three."

"Okay. Get in touch with Andrew and let him know I have a few minutes now. I need to put the finishing touches on my notes for the chancellor's meeting, but I can squeeze him in before that."

"Would you like me to get your bulletproof vest from the cleaners?"

"Ha!" Nate gave a hearty laugh. "I'm afraid it will take more than that to fight off the dreaded Dr. Andrew R. Bellinger." He gestured toward his office. "A padded cell might be useful, though."

Margaret chuckled. "Sometimes I think that man's name should have been Belligerent rather than Bellinger." She clucked her tongue. "I'll let him know he has to be up here in ten minutes." A sly grin slipped across her face. "I'll try not to trip him when he walks by my desk."

"Don't do that," Nate said. "People will start to talk about how all the computer science professors are being injured."

"That's true. It really isn't funny, is it? Have you gotten any update on Dr. Malone?"

"I called and talked to his nurse yesterday. He's fussing and fuming with the doctors about having to stay at home to rest, but they're adamant. The head injury, combined with the serious injuries to his spine and legs, can't be ignored. He's lucky to be alive."

"Have the police found anything?"

"Not that I know of. They've been asking a lot of questions, and they said they'd let me know if they uncovered anything, but so far nothing."

"It's awful. Dr. Malone was no fun to work for, but I wouldn't wish an accident like that on anybody. Do the doctors have any idea when he can return to work?"

"His nurse says they're unsure if he'll ever be able to come back full time. It's a day-by-day process." He shrugged. "In the meantime, I get the pleasure of being interim chairman and taking all the—um—suggestions offered by our faculty." He shook his head with a wry grin. "I sure hope Malone recovers soon. I never realized what a pain it is to be a department chair. It's nothing I would ever aspire to."

* * *

Nate took a seat at his desk in the vice-chairman's office. The university president had suggested he move into the chairman's office as an affirmation of his authority, but he wouldn't do that. His own office as vice-chair was not as grand, but it was a comfortable cave for him to prepare lectures and meet with graduate students. And the other faculty members wouldn't think he was trying to boost himself by moving into the chairman's office.

The other faculty members. As soon as the new chancellor had asked him to take over Malone's position, the relationships with his colleagues had changed. Some seemed happy to have him as their leader. Others grew more guarded in conversations, and some were outright hostile, especially

Andrew Bellinger. Nate had heard himself being referred to by the young professor as "that stupid carrot-top."

It seemed every relationship he had on campus was now filtered through this new position. Even Mr. Tyme, the librarian, had changed. Mr. Tyme had been a great respecter of the upper administrators and department chairs. After Nate became interim chairman, Mr. Tyme seemed to want to cultivate a relationship, and he had asked Nate's help to review some kind of code he had found.

Nate picked up the printed outline for the upcoming meeting with the new chancellor and jotted a few notes in the margins. The new man had to understand the need to keep a highly respected faculty and a strong program even in the shadow of the recent financial crisis. Their graduate students were top-notch. Malone was a task master and an unpleasant man to work with, but he had made the computer science department competitive with the best in the country. Nate had to keep it going.

There was a loud banging at the door, and Nate felt his jaw tense for the meeting ahead. "Come in."

Andrew Bellinger opened the door and firmly shut it behind him. Although he'd been on the faculty for several years, Andrew looked like a grad student with his long hair, blue jeans, and T-shirt. He strode to the front of Nate's desk and stood with feet apart and arms folded over his chest. There was nothing on his face but bitter frustration.

Nate felt the color rising in his face as he sensed the acrid vibes coming from the younger man. This was going to be a repeat of the last meeting, but he doubted there would be any difference in Andrew's reaction. "Have a seat, Andrew."

Andrew dropped into the chair opposite and continued to stare bullets into Nate. "We need to discuss my situation here," he said. "Malone would never consider me for tenure, but he's out of the picture now. You're in charge and you can put me up for tenure with a stroke of your pen. I've got all the background and experience I need. I've updated my CV and emailed it to you, so it should be an easy decision."

"I appreciate your position, Andrew." Nate carefully laid his pen on the desk and interlaced his fingers. "And you've made it very clear how much you want this to happen."

"I've taught multiple courses every semester, and my student evaluation reports have been excellent." With his right index finger, he touched each finger of his left hand as he listed his accomplishments. "I've published in several respected journals." He paused and waved one hand toward the door. "And I was even willing to put together that stupid cryptography exhibit when nobody else would take it on."

"There's nothing stupid about the exhibit, Andrew." Nate frowned at the younger man. "It's good public relations to have people from the community drop by, and there's always an interest in puzzles and codes. I appreciate your hard work."

Andrew snorted and shrugged.

Penterson leaned forward on his desk. "As far as your performance as a faculty member, I agree you've been an impressive asset to the department. However, I've made it clear I won't make any major decisions until Dr. Malone is able to consult with me." Nate fought to remain calm while he saw Andrew's expression grow even darker. "It's not a question of my confidence in you. You're an excellent professor, and your research record is one of the best in the department. However, I'm only interim chair, and I won't take on the responsibility of a decision for tenure."

"Everybody knows Malone is out for good. His injuries are serious, and the big boys want you to take over. All you have to do is say the word and it's done."

"Andrew, I appreciate what you're saying, but there's no use arguing. I won't take action until Malone's situation is settled."

Bellinger stood defiantly. "You're no better than he was." His jaw clamped shut and he stomped out.

Chapter Nine

PHIL DOESN'T LIKE IT

Kathryn approached the receptionist in the front hall of Warren's Auto Repair office. "Hi, Rebecca. Is Phil in?"

The young woman looked up and smiled. "Hi, Kathryn. Yes, he's here. I think he's in his office."

Kate walked quickly down the long hallway that led to the repair floor. A year ago, she wouldn't have believed she would love the smell of motor oil and mechanical grease. But those things had come to represent the amazing man who had left an Ivy League university to return to Bellevue and open a business to support his mother and sister after his father's sudden death.

One in a million.

She stopped just outside his office and took a deep breath. "Hey," she said as she peeked around the corner of the office door at Phil, who was shuffling through papers on his desk.

"Hey, beautiful." He looked up with the sly smile on his face she had come to associate with a warm welcome. A very warm welcome.

"Come here," he said. "And close the door." His blue eyes sparkled. "Lock it."

As the owner of the repair shop, Phil rarely worked on cars himself, but he always had a blue grease rag in the back pocket of his jeans. Kate felt a familiar tug at her heart as she watched him stand and move toward her.

She locked the door behind her and found herself in his arms.

Phil lifted her chin. "I've been sitting here worrying about why Reverend Whitefield wanted to talk to you. Don't tell me you're going to get involved with another murder investigation."

"Well ..."

"I'd better sit down for this." He sank into one of the chairs in front of his desk and pulled her onto his lap. "At least we can be comfortable while you tell me the reason you're going to risk your life again."

She kissed him long and sweetly. Then she stood. "I can't talk to you when I'm sitting on your lap. You get me all discombobulated."

"Ha. You've never been discombobulated in your life. But I hope I can at least take your mind away from murder investigations for a while."

"You're pretty good at that. But this is important."

"So are you." He locked his eyes on hers. "And that's why I don't want you getting involved again."

Kate leaned against the desk and frowned down at him.

"I recognize that look," he said. "You're going to tell me you need to help the police find a murderer." He shook his head. "You know I don't like this."

"Phil, I realize how you feel, and I love you for it. But Reverend and Mrs. Whitefield have done so much for me, I can't let him down. Besides, he doesn't want me to investigate a murder."

She propped herself on the desk and filled him in on everything she and Cece had learned. "So you see, all we have to do is figure out the code on the prayer request." She chewed on her lip. "But there is one thing that's worrying me."

"What?"

"The little girls have suddenly attached themselves to Cece and me."

"Reen and her cousin?"

"Yes. Reen jumped to the conclusion that there's a murder, and she's already talking about helping us find a killer. I need to talk to her father about getting her distracted from this thing."

"If you think you can turn Reen Penterson's attention to something else, you are dead wrong. There's only one person I know who's more stubborn than she is."

"Who?"

He pulled her back down into his lap. "You know who. And we both know you're going to get involved in this thing until you figure out if someone actually killed Mr. Tyme." He shook his head. "You know, you're the stubbornest woman I've ever known."

Kate put a look of mock surprise on her face. "And have you known many women, Mr. Warren?"

"I've known a few." The sly smile slipped across his face again. "But I never knew anybody like you." He ran his index finger down her arm and the smile dropped off his face, replaced by a frown. "I'd like to talk to Commissioner Blake about this. Maybe he'd be willing to reopen the investigation. Is that all right with you?"

"Sure. That'd be great."

"I don't know how we're ever going to reconcile your habit of solving crimes with my concern for your safety."

"I'll be careful. Honest."

"You'd better be," he said as he pulled her face down to his and kissed her again.

Chapter Ten

PHIL GOES TO THE COPS

Detective Carlioni looked up from his desk when he heard the tap at the door. He turned to his partner. "That must be him, Mac."

Detective MacMillan closed his laptop and walked to the office door. He opened it and Phil Warren stepped in.

"Hey, guys. Thanks for seeing me."

"No problem, Mr. Warren," Carlioni said. "We're always glad to see you." He motioned to a chair in front of his desk. "What's up?"

"Call me Phil." He took a seat, put his elbows on the arms of the chair, and steepled his fingers together. "I called Commissioner Blake, but his secretary says he's on vacation for a while."

"Yeah. Blake had so much vacation time built up, the administration said he had to take a month of it or lose it, so he booked a cruise with his wife. It's their fortieth wedding anniversary." Carlioni shrugged. "Blake needed a rest. He and the mayor don't always see eye-to-eye on how to handle investigations, and I think he was glad to get away for a while."

"Who's taking his place?"

Carlioni scrunched his face into a scowl. "The powers that be brought in a temporary replacement. Sam Simpkins."

"How's he working out?" Phil asked.

"It's not a 'he,'" MacMillan said. "It's a 'she.'"

"Sam Simpkins is a woman?"

"Yep." Carlioni sighed. "Samantha Simpkins. She's a one-woman, full-speed-ahead, get-the-job-done dynamo."

MacMillan chuckled. "She's climbing the blue ladder, and you'd better not get in her way."

"The blue ladder?" Phil asked.

"Law enforcement for upper management." Carlioni snorted. "The big bosses at the state level love her. She hits the ground running and rolls over everything in her path. I get the feeling they're grooming her to take over when Blake retires."

"I didn't know Commissioner Blake was going to retire."

"He hasn't said anything to us, but you never know. He's getting close to that age." Carlioni shook his head. "And this past year has taken a lot out of him."

"Yeah. We've all had some pretty exciting adventures. A lot more than we bargained for, that's for sure." Phil stood and paced in a little circle. Then he stopped and looked at the two detectives. "I need somebody to help me. Maybe I can talk to this Simpkins."

"Good luck on that," MacMillan said. "Word is out that she won't get involved in anything that doesn't come down from above. Strictly by the book, and only works on things that will get her promoted." He gave a resigned smiled. "What do you need help with?"

Phil pressed his lips together. "It has to do with Kathryn."

Carlioni and MacMillan exchanged glances. MacMillan leaned against the filing cabinet.

"Uh-oh," Carlioni said. "Don't tell me she got herself mixed up in another murder case."

"Well, yes and no." Phil smiled weakly.

Carlioni raised an eyebrow. "That's an answer we hear a lot from lawyers, but I'm surprised to get it from you. Why don't you just tell us what's going on."

"Reverend Whitefield has asked Kathryn to look into Mr. Tyme's death. Or at least to try to decipher a code on a slip of paper he thinks has something to do with it. I don't want her fooling around with another thing that can put her in danger."

"We didn't handle the Tyme investigation," MacMillan said. "It was all done by the fire department and the boys in blue. I heard they ruled the death an accident."

"That's right. But if there was more to it, I don't want Kathryn to be in the middle of it. I was hoping the police would reopen the investigation. Then Kathryn wouldn't have to be involved. Can you fellas help?"

"We can't do anything without authorization from Simpkins," MacMillan said. "Once the report came back that it was an accidental death, she checked it off her list. Every time she does this"—he made a gesture in the air like a big check mark—"it counts as one more accomplishment for her."

Carlioni picked up a mechanical pencil from his desk and twirled it around his fingers. "Look. We all know what a great person Kathryn is. She's smart and dedicated and wants to right every wrong." He dropped the pencil back on the desk. "But if there was any foul play involved with Tyme's death, we don't want her getting mixed up in it. We can talk to Simpkins and see if she'll give us a shot at it."

"Thanks guys. That's all I'm asking." Phil walked to the door, put his hand on the knob, and turned back to face them. "All I want is to keep Kathryn safe."

* * *

Carlioni dropped the receiver back in its cradle and made a thumbs-down gesture.

"She's not going for it?" MacMillan asked.

"She said she's satisfied with the police report, and we need to take care of our own cases." He picked up a stress ball from his desk and squeezed it. "I don't like this, Mac. Blake would have let us look into it if he thought we had a hunch."

"Yeah, I agree. Maybe we can do a little snooping on our own."

"That's the other problem," Carlioni said.

"Huh?"

"Simpkins said she'd better not hear of us trying to sneak around on our own. She said that would constitute insubordination." He squeezed the stress ball viciously. "Can you believe that woman? She's threatening to fire us if we look into Mr. Tyme's death."

Chapter Eleven

THE COAL CLUE

Kathryn inhaled the enticing aroma of sautéed chicken that drifted into the living room from the kitchen. Cece stuck her head around the corner. "Fried rice or white?" she said.

Kate looked up from her laptop. "Definitely fried," she said. "And it smells delicious. I sure am glad one of us knows how to cook."

Cece disappeared back into the kitchen. "It's a simple division of labor," she called out. "You break the code and find a murderer. I make dinner."

"Deal," Kate said. "I'm calling this the Coal Clue."

"Good idea." Cece's voice floated back from the kitchen. "Giving something a name is the first step to getting to know it."

Kate put her feet on the ottoman and leaned back against the sofa cushions, her laptop resting on her legs. She opened the document, typed the code into a decipher app, and stared at it. "Okay, Mr. Coal Clue. What can you tell me about yourself?" She poked the enter key and the app returned "No results."

"Huh." If it was a simple substitution code, the app would have found it. She stared at the code.

WAPSPAHIODDPSABEMOKIKITIODIL

Maybe each letter is the beginning of a word. "Why are pointy shoes painful and harmful ..." *Hmm.*

She opened the book on codes she had picked up at the bookstore and scanned through the first chapters. She spent half an hour trying different means of breaking the code.

"How's it going?" Cece brought out two plates of steaming chicken stir-fry and placed them on the coffee table. "I thought we could just eat in here and talk about the problem. Hold on, I'll get the silverware and napkins." She headed back to the kitchen.

Kate put her laptop aside. "I think you're doing a much better job with dinner than I am with code breaking."

"No success?" Cece placed napkins and silverware on the coffee table.

"Nothing. I'm using this code book." She tapped the cover. "But I'm not getting anywhere." She took a bite of Cece's concoction. "Mm. On the other hand, you're a genius. Did you get this out of a recipe book?"

"Nope. Sometimes you can make the best meals just by being creative with what you find in the refrigerator."

"Never worked for me." Kate grinned.

Cece chewed in silence for a minute. "Do you suppose the code could just be random letters? Maybe they don't mean anything."

"Possible. But why would somebody do that?" She put her fork down and picked up the slip of paper with the code. "I thought it might be a sentence with each letter being the first letter in a word." She handed it to Cece. "I came up with some pretty silly phrases."

"That could be a great party game." Cece laughed and took a swallow of water.

"Yeah. Too bad it isn't a game, huh?" They both fell silent again.

"Why do you suppose it says 'God Remembers'? Does God ever forget?" Kate asked.

"No, but there are places in Scripture that use that phrase. The Bible says 'God remembered Noah' after the flood. He hadn't forgotten about him, but God was going to act. Maybe he was going to change something about Noah's life."

"Something sure got changed about Mr. Tyme's life."

They fell silent again and Cece pushed food around on her plate. "I think Reverend Whitefield is right. Somebody is trying to tell us something, but if we can't decipher the code, we may never know what it is."

"And we won't know if there's a killer on the loose."

Chapter Twelve

THE CLOCKWORKS

Kate and Cece arrived at the quad in front of the bell tower and found the two girls waiting for them. Joanie was sitting on the bench, swinging her legs back and forth while she picked petals off a daisy. Reen was turning cartwheels and trying to stand on her hands.

Cece clapped her hands. "Good afternoon, friends! It looks like we're all here for today's tour of the bell tower and lecture on the internal workings of time."

Joanie giggled and ran to Cece to hold her hand.

Reen pulled a notebook out of her pocket. "I'm going to take notes on everything Cece teaches us so I can write an article about clocks," she said. "I bet they'll pay me for it." She unclipped a pen and flipped the cover of the notebook back.

"That's a great idea, Reen," Kate said. "This will be a special tour for all of us." She pointed to the clock, and they all looked up at the hands that were embedded in the rough-hewn stone of the tower. Above the clock, the tower that housed the bell and gong arm was open on four sides so the chime could be heard all over campus.

Kate looked back down at the others. "But first we have to unlock the door to the tower. Reverend Whitefield said Mr. Venero would meet us here to open the door."

Venero appeared from around the side of the building. "I'm here," he said in a low voice. "I don't normally open the door to the tower, but the reverend said it was all right to do it for you." He took a chain with a set of keys off his belt and flipped through them.

"That's a lot of keys you got there," Cece said.

Venero frowned but didn't speak as he clinked each key over. When he found the one he wanted, he slipped it into the door and pulled it open.

"You must be pretty special to rate a master key," Cece said.

"Nothing special about me." Venero gestured toward the darkness inside. "Be careful. Steps are hard."

"We're not going to get locked in, are we?" Cece asked.

"No. I have to stay with you. University rules."

Joanie held tight to Cece's hand. "I'm afraid of the dark," she said quietly.

Venero reached in and flipped a switch, and lights illuminated the stone stairs leading up to the belfry. "Nothing to be afraid of. Just be careful on the stairs." He held the door open and motioned them in.

"I'm not afraid," Reen said. But she reached for Kate's hand.

"Okay, team. Here we go!" Kate led the way and the four entered the door and followed Mr. Venero up the stone steps to the level of the bell.

* * *

At the top of the stairs, Kate stepped into the bell room and felt her eyes almost bug out at the sight of the enormous object in the center of the room.

The others followed Kate into the room. "Wow. What a huge bell!" Reen said, and her mouth dropped open in awe.

Kathryn nodded. "That's amazing. I never realized how big it is." She gestured toward the arm suspended from the top of the bell with a hammer at its end. "I guess the hammer strikes the bell on the hour. Is that right, Mr. Venero?"

Venero's voice sounded louder in the small space of the bell room. "Yes."

Joanie pulled at Cece's hand and pointed to the corner. "I saw a mouse. It ran inside that hole." She wrinkled her nose and moved as close as she could to Cece. "I don't like mice. They're dirty."

"Sometimes there are little critters that live in bell towers," Cece said, "but a mouse won't hurt us."

Reen was staring at the large bell in the center of the room. "How does the hammer know how many times to hit the bell?"

Cece stepped up. "That's a great question, and I can explain it. Let's take a look at the clock gears." She led them to a locked plexiglass door.

"You can't go in there," Venero said. "Only clock repairmen are allowed."

"That's okay," Cece said. "I can describe how it works from here." They gathered around her. "I was reading about this clock last night. It's an old mechanism that was left to the university by a donor who was a watchmaker. He wanted to preserve the mechanical style of clocks, so he agreed to fund the building of the bell tower if they would preserve the old clockworks."

She pointed to the gears. "See the gears? They're turned by the pendulum that swings down below."

"I hear it ticking," Joanie said.

"Good!" Cece smiled at the little redhead. "You're hearing the anchor. See, it's the little seesaw that rocks back and forth to slow down the escape wheel."

"I see it!" Reen pointed. "See, Joanie, it's right there." She took out her phone and snapped a picture.

"All the gears work together," Cece said. "The little gear turns all the way around once a minute. You can hear it click every time it completes a cycle. Listen."

They all got quiet as the gear approached the top and made a loud click. "I heard it!" Joanie jumped up and down and clapped her hands.

"Good," Cece said. "And the big gear turns once an hour. Then it causes the hammer to strike the bell."

"I like the gears," Joanie said.

"I can tell you a story about the gears," Kathryn said, and they all turned toward her. "The reason they put up the barrier so you can't get to the mechanism is because ten or fifteen years ago some students decided to stop the clock."

"How could they stop it?" Joanie asked.

"Back then there wasn't the plexiglass barrier. The boys wanted to stop the clock so the bell wouldn't chime, and they could skip final exams."

"Wow. That's brilliant," Reen said. "Did they get away with it?"

"They stopped the clock, all right, and caused all kinds of confusion on campus. But in the end, it was worse for them than if they had taken their exams."

"Why? What happened?"

"They got kicked out of school and the university built the barrier so nobody could stop the clock from chiming after that."

"I want to see the hammer hit the bell," Reen said. "Is it going to chime soon?"

Cece looked at her watch. "We've just got a few minutes until the top of the hour. Then the hammer will strike the bell twice for two o'clock." She looked down at the children. "Isn't this fun?"

Reen started to move toward the bell in the center of the room.

"No." Mr. Venero had been standing rigidly to the side, listening to Cece and Kate, but now he stepped in front of Reen to block her path. "No one's allowed to get close to the bell. It's too dangerous." He pointed to the arm. "If you get in the way of the arm, you could be hurt."

Kate noticed Mr. Venero was sweating even though it was cool in the tower. She put her hand on Reen's shoulder. "Mr. Venero is right. It could be dangerous. We'll watch it from here."

Each time the minute gear completed a cycle, they heard a loud click. "The next time it moves," Cece said, "should be on the hour. Then we'll see how everything works."

There was a click followed by a louder click when the large gear moved into place. They all watched as the bell arm, which had hung lifeless in front of the bell, began to move. It swung out slowly, paused, and then forcefully struck the bell with a loud clang that reverberated in the tower. They all put their hands over their ears as the arm swung out and hammered the side of the bell again.

"Wow. That was amazing," Reen said. "Can we stay up here until three o'clock to see it again?"

"No." Mr. Venero frowned. "You have to leave now. It's too dangerous for you to be up here."

Reen made an appeal to Kathryn with her eyes. Kate shook her head. "Mr. Venero is right. Now that you know how the bell tower works, you can write your paper. You can even include the pictures you took."

Chapter Thirteen

BIG GIRL STRATEGY

"Taking the girls to see the bell tower clock was a great idea," Kate said and settled on the bench that was built into the side wall of the clock tower.

"Do you suppose they got anything out of my little lecture about clocks?" Cece asked as she plopped on the bench next to her sister.

"I think they did. Joanie liked it, and Reen was taking notes the whole time." She chuckled. "I bet she goes home and googles 'clock towers' to write her paper."

"Yep. She's a smart one. Do you think we got them distracted from Mr. Tyme's death?"

"I'll check with Reen's father later." Kate shook her head. "Looks like we may have solved one problem, but we've got a bigger problem on our hands."

"What's that?"

Kate pulled at her ponytail. "I need to get some help to solve the code. It's too sophisticated for me."

"Okay, Sherlock, how are we going to find out more about Mr. Tyme without letting people know we're investigating his death?"

"I've been thinking about that. We need to come up with a cover story, so nobody suspects us of trying to get information on Mr. Tyme."

They sat in silence while the robins and blue jays sang and fussed in the birch trees. The morning breeze had died down, and Kate felt the heat radiating from the tower wall. She gazed at the buildings that stood sentry over the grassy quad. To her left, stone lions guarded the library and its thousands of books.

She had been a kindergartner when her father held her hand and led her up those imposing steps and into that grand building. He had guided her through the aisles, and she had touched the spines of the books in childish delight. Maybe she could find something in the library to help her solve the mystery of the codes. *A mystery of codes.*

Suddenly, Kate jumped up and snapped her fingers. "I've got it. Oh, Cece, I just had a great idea!"

"Uh-oh." Cece raised her eyebrows. "I've seen that look on your face before, and it usually involves something unhealthy." She crossed her arms over her chest and leaned back. "Okay, let's have it."

Kate paced back and forth in front of the bench. "I'll say I'm doing research for an author who's writing a mystery."

"I hate to admit it," Cece said, "but this sounds interesting. Keep going."

"The idea of the mystery is that everything is based on coded messages, and the author has asked me to do the research on cryptography for her. That will give me an excuse to interview faculty in the computer science department who may know something. I can find a way to work Mr. Tyme into the conversations." She grinned at Cece. "What do you think?"

"I think it sounds intriguing. In fact, it's perfect. But suppose they want to meet the author. Then what are you going to do?"

"No problem. I'll just say she's from Canada and we're working online with each other."

Cece shook her head. "That could still be a problem. Somebody could look her up and find out she doesn't exist."

"Hmm." Kate frowned. "You're right. Maybe it wasn't such a great idea after all."

Cece stood and her face transformed into a huge grin. "Actually," she said, "I know an author we could use."

"You do?" Kate said. "Who is it?"

"Me."

"You? You're not an author. Nobody would buy that." Kate shook her head. "We need a real author."

"No, you don't understand. I can do my superpower thing. Remember how many times I've been in costume and you didn't recognize me?" She held her hands out, palms up. "We can set me up as the mystery writer. You know mystery writers are all weird." She made a circular motion with her finger around one ear. "It would be the performance of a lifetime!"

"Do you really think we could pull it off?"

Cece nodded eagerly. "Absolutely. I can already envision myself as an eccentric old woman. Agatha Christie reborn." Her smile faded. "But they might look up my character's writing credentials, and we can't make those up."

"True." Kate bit on her bottom lip. "But we can say it's her first book. She's from Canada and she's traveling around the US to get ideas for her book. She's always wanted to write a mystery, and now she has the time to do it. She decided to set it on a university campus." She gestured around her. "It's perfect."

"We can create an email account for her and even give her an author website." Cece giggled and hugged herself. Then she stopped and frowned. "But why did she pick you to do the research?"

"Um. Good question." Kate shook her head and thought for a minute. "I've got it. She's the elderly aunt of a friend of mine from college, and my friend recommended me because he said I have a lot of expertise solving puzzles and things. And she can't afford an expert, so I said I'd do the research for free."

"Suppose they look up your friend."

"Who would do that? If somebody asks, we'll say my friend's name was —um—John Taylor. There must be a million John Taylors in the world. No way they could check on it."

"Okay. Count me in. Let's think of a good name for our mystery writer."

Kate grinned. "You're the expert on names. You come up with one."

"Hmm." Cece looked out over the campus. "I've got it. We'll call her Rose Ramen."

"Ramen? What kind of name is that? Does it have a meaning?"

"Of course. The Latin word for mystery is *sacramentum*. I always thought that was interesting because it's where the word 'sacrament' comes from. The exact center of the word is 'ramen,' so that'll be her name. She's at the middle of the mystery!"

"I love it, and you're brilliant," Kate said. "But why Rose?"

"It's from *The Name of the Rose*, the great mystery by Umberto Eco." Cece giggled. "Ha! This is perfect. I'll start putting together the outfit this afternoon. This is going to be my best part ever!"

As the two girls hugged each other, the tower clock's gears moved. There was a loud click, and the powerful bell rang out three times.

Chapter Fourteen

THE UNIVERSITY LIBRARY

I figure librarians know the most about murder. After all, they're locked up all day with a bunch of stale books and have to deal with people who don't know how to use the computers.

Miss Culberson is the university librarian I like the most. She always helps me, even when I pester her with questions. Today, she was leaning down behind the information desk when Joanie and I got there.

"Hi, Miss Culberson."

She looked up and peered at me over her half-size, pink-rimmed plastic glasses. She always wears the same ones, and they're on a black bungee cord that holds them when she takes them off and drops them down. But she never takes them off. Maybe she thinks the cord makes her look cool. It doesn't.

Miss Culberson's face is pale, and she has short, wavy blonde hair with gray roots. She's not much taller than I am, and I'm sure she doesn't get enough exercise because her arms wiggle when she's wearing short sleeves like she is today.

"Hello, girls. I haven't seen you since school got out." Her voice is high and crisp. Every word seems important. I guess they teach them that in librarian school. "I'm glad you're here now. Reen, I have some new mystery novels you're going to like."

"Thanks, Miss Culberson, but I don't have time for pleasure reading anymore."

"Oh? And what are you so busy with?"

There are two kinds of adults in the world. The kind that doesn't pay you any attention and the kind that pretends they're interested in what you have to say. You know, the ones that give you a little half smile that means *You're just a kid and don't know anything, but I'm going to be nice to you so I don't ruin your psyche.* Miss Culberson is definitely the second kind, but I like her anyway.

"I've decided to become an investigative reporter," I said with a sharp nod of the head to add emphasis. "I'm interested in finding the truth, no matter where it takes me." I had the feeling she was stifling a smile.

"I see," she said. "That's very commendable." She uses that word a lot. I had to look it up when I was a little kid because she always told me everything I did was commendable. It means "good."

"And what are you investigating today?"

"I can't tell you the nature of my investigation, but I have some questions you might be able to help me with." I took my notebook and pen out. They make me look official.

"Wonderful. I'll give you all the help I can." She moved some books to the side and sat down behind the desk. She adjusted the pink bow on her lacey white blouse and leaned her arms on the desk so she and I were on eye level. I like it when I can look an adult right in the face. Makes me feel like we're equal. "Now, what do you want to know?"

I decided to use the element of surprise. You know, throw something out unexpected-like to see their reaction. I locked my eyes onto her face. "What do you know about Mr. Tyme's death?"

Her pale face went completely white, her eyes got big and round, and her spectacles fell down onto their bungee cord. I guess there's a first time for everything. She sat straight up in her chair and moved a few more books around. I thought maybe she was buying time so she wouldn't have to answer me. Sometimes when I bother her, she'll suddenly remember she has some books to reshelve, but that didn't happen. She put her glasses back on and looked at me again. "Mr. Tyme?" Her voice shot up about an octave. "Why are you asking about him?"

"He died. And I'm going to find out what happened." There. I said it out loud. I thought maybe she'd scream and run out of the room. Or maybe she'd admit she murdered him because he was going to hire a younger woman to replace her. Or maybe she'd just call my dad and tell him to come pick me up.

Her face became stern, more than ever before, and her cheeks turned the same color pink as her glasses.

"Reen, you shouldn't be investigating a death." Ah. The *you're-too-young-to-know-anything* approach. "That was a gruesome thing and not one a young girl should be concerned with. If you want to be an investigative reporter, I suggest you look into something else." She picked up a newspaper lying next to the stack of books. "Here. There's a big story in yesterday's paper about how the school system is funded. You could investigate that and find some positive ways to help the community. Looking into a terrible accident isn't a good idea."

I leaned against the desk, trying to look older and nonchalant like reporters did in the old movies. "Sorry, Miss Culberson, but this is my assignment. If you won't talk to me, I'll find someone who will." I looked down at my notebook and pretended to review my notes. "You know, it may not have been an accident."

She gasped and got up and walked around the desk. Her pink shoes made little clicking noises on the wood floor. I'm surprised librarians are allowed to wear high heels. Shouldn't they always wear Hush Puppies? And who wears pink shoes anyway? When she looked down at me, I knew this was going to be one of those don't-go-there conversations. But she's not much taller than I am, so she's not very scary. Not like Mrs. Toussaint.

"Reen, I appreciate your curiosity, but this is a serious subject for a child. I'll have to talk to your father before I give you any information about Mr. Tyme."

The shock approach wasn't working as well as I had hoped. I needed a better plan of attack. "We don't have to talk about the fire," I said, and I put the flummoxed expression on my face. That's the one adults respond to best when they don't want to hurt your feelings. But I didn't whine. They don't like it when you whine, and you'll lose all the progress you made along the way. "I'd just like to know what he was like. You know, how he was to work for, what he liked to read about, his daily habits."

"Clarence Tyme was a dear friend, and I don't mind telling you about what a nice man he was and how well we worked together." She held up her index finger and wagged it at me. "But nothing about the accident, understood?"

"Oh, yes, Miss Culberson. I understand." I tried to look like a puppy dog eagerly waiting for a pat on the head. She went back to her chair, and I smiled on the inside. I might win the Pulitzer Prize.

* * *

Lillian Culberson took her pink-rimmed glasses off and let them drop on the cord around her neck. She had given Reen a pleasant little story about Clarence Tyme. She had said he was a nice man and a good person to work for. They got along very well, and she had always had the highest regard for him. He didn't have any enemies and he died in a sad accident. End of story. Then she had given Reen and Joanie a list of children's books and shooed them to the other end of the library.

She watched the two young girls walk away, and she felt her face grow hot at the memory of Mr. Tyme. Everyone thought he was such a lovely person, but only she knew what a tyrant he was to work for. Every suggestion she'd ever made about the library had to be discussed at length, and he hardly approved any of them. A lovely man, indeed!

She felt the heat rising in her cheeks, and she looked around the large expanse of the library to see if anyone would witness her face flushing red. At this time of year, with the spring semester over and the summer classes not yet started, there were few visitors to the library. Good. It would give her time to think and work things out.

She had been so careful when the police questioned her about Mr. Tyme. She had answered their questions honestly. She just hadn't given the whole story.

But what if the police decide it was more than an accidental fire and came around asking questions again? What if they found out about the argument? Could someone else have overheard it? What about that silly piece of paper?

She put her head in her hands and tried to remember every detail about that night. He had told her to go home a little early because he had some things he wanted to finish up at the library. He said he was working on the last details of a puzzle and wanted to be alone. And then they'd had that terrible altercation.

The police might find out that she and Mr. Tyme didn't get along, and that she had access to the back door of the library just outside Mr. Tyme's office.

Lillian Culberson gripped the edge of the desk and took a sharp breath. How could she stop Reen and Joanie from their nonsense?

Chapter Fifteen

LITTLE GIRL RESEARCH

"Why do we have to use a library computer?" Joanie pushed a chair up next to mine. "Why can't we go to your house and use yours?"

"Because somebody can trace us if we use mine. This way, they don't know who's doing the searching." We found one of the library computers way over in the corner away from traffic. "We have to be covert."

"Oh." She pulled her chair closer and climbed on it. "What's covert?"

"It means we have to keep it a secret."

"I'm good at keeping secrets." Joanie put her finger to her lips like she was shushing somebody. "What are we going to search for?"

"Today, we'll just do the obvious. We'll google Mr. Tyme and see what we can find out."

I typed "Tyme" in the search box, and we got over twelve million hits. None of the ones on the first page looked like they had anything to do with our Mr. Tyme. "Hmm," I said, "let's try this."

I typed "Mr. Tyme" in the search box, and it got better. Only two million hits. But the first page still didn't say anything about *our* Mr. Tyme.

"It isn't working," Joanie said. She's really good at stating the obvious.

"Wait. What did Miss Culberson call him?" I fingered the keyboard, trying to remember. "She said 'Dear' somebody."

Joanie has this amazing talent. She remembers everything. She pursed her lips the way she does when she's trying to think. Then her face lit up. "I remember. She made me think of the circus when she said it."

"The circus? His name wasn't Lion Tamer Tyme, was it?"

Joanie laughed out loud and then clapped her hand over her mouth. "No, silly," she said in her loudish way of whispering. "It was that clown."

I shrugged my shoulders and sighed. We had just left the universe of rational thought.

Joanie leaned forward so I could hear her whisper. "You remember when Mrs. Toussaint wanted us to watch an episode of *The Howdy Doody Show*. It had Clarabell the Clown."

"You think Mr. Tyme's name was Clarabell?"

Joanie giggled and shook her head so hard her ponytails wrapped around and slapped her in the face. "It *sounded* like Clarabell." She looked at me and raised her eyebrows. "Don't you remember?"

I could see this was turning into one of those Joanie-in-control moments. "No. And I don't want to guess. Just tell me."

"It rhymes with 'parents,'" she said.

"Parents?" I noodled on that for a minute. Joanie's teacher had her class writing poems this year in school and now she's all about rhyming things. "Oh, I remember now. Clarence!" I'll never understand how Joanie's brain works, but I have to admit, it can be a thing of beauty. "You're a genius!"

Joanie rocked back in her chair and hugged herself. I typed "Clarence Tyme" into the search box. Ten thousand hits, but the first page was all about our Mr. Tyme. Pay dirt.

* * *

"Whoa. Look at that!" My fingers froze above the keyboard when the picture of Mr. Tyme popped up.

"What?" Joanie leaned closer.

"It says he was sixty-eight years old." I looked over at Joanie. "I didn't know people that old were allowed to work, did you?"

Joanie bit on her bottom lip. "I don't know. My Gramma Finelson is old, and she still works."

Live and learn. I scrolled down the page. "It says he won a prize in a crossword puzzle contest and he was a good librarian." I scrolled some more. "Look. Here's a story about the fire." I clicked on the link.

"What does it say?"

I read fast. "The police think Mr. Tyme fell down in his office and hit his head. Then his cigarette caught everything on fire." I scrunched up my face and tried to think. "Sounds like the police are taking the easy way out. That way they don't have to do any work."

"Maybe they're right," Joanie said.

"But maybe it wasn't an accident." I turned around in my chair to face her. "Let's suppose somebody killed Mr. Tyme. How would they do it?"

"Hmm." Joanie got off her chair and made a frowny face, like she was thinking really hard. "Maybe Mr. Tyme got in a fight with somebody, and the other guy pushed him, and Mr. Tyme hit his head. Then the other guy ran away and didn't realize the cigarette was going to start a fire."

I looked at Joanie in surprise. Maybe her detective skills were coming along after all.

"But there's a problem with that." I pointed to the article on the screen. "It says here the door was locked with a dead bolt. If somebody just ran out of the room, the door couldn't lock itself."

"What's a dead bolt?"

"You know, it's one of those locks you have to turn, and it moves a bolt into the other side of the door. It means Mr. Tyme must have locked the door from the inside." I rested my chin on my hand to help me think.

"But if he locked it from the inside, it must have been an accident like they said."

"But somebody could have locked the door with a key from the outside." I jumped out of my chair. "That's it. Somebody hit Mr. Tyme on the head, ran out, and locked the office. Mr. Tyme fell down when he got hit, and his cigarette set the room on fire."

Joanie paced down the aisle and her ponytails bobbed up and down like corks when fish are nibbling at the bait. She turned around and bobbed back to me. "Who would have a key to Mr. Tyme's office?"

We looked at each other, our mouths fell open, and we both gasped at the same time. "Miss Culberson!"

Chapter Sixteen

MR. TYME'S OFFICE

Kathryn followed the big policeman as they descended the stairs to the basement of the library. "Thank you for meeting us here, Mr. Olssen. I realize this is outside your normal duties."

Officer Olssen was a huge man, at least six foot four. Kate guessed he had Swedish ancestry with his blond hair and pale complexion. "Reverend Whitefield asked me to show you Mr. Tyme's office, and I'm always happy to do a favor for him. He's my minister, you know."

They arrived at the base of the stairs, and Olssen used his key to open the door to Mr. Tyme's office. "Watch your step."

Cece poked her head into the burned-out office. "What a mess," she said and stepped back. "Why haven't they cleaned this up before now?"

Olssen shrugged. "I heard the university is having some budget problems, and they're waiting until the start of their fiscal year to completely renovate the room."

"Were you the lead investigator on this case?" Kate asked.

"Yes, ma'am." He brushed at some of the ash residue on the frame of the door. "Ugly business. And a real shame for Mr. Tyme."

"Did you know him?"

"He was a deacon at my church, but I didn't know him well. People we interviewed said he was a real nice man. But he sure wasn't lucky, was he?"

"What do you mean?" Kate folded her arms over her chest.

"He was down here by himself after hours and had locked himself in his office."

"How do you know he locked himself in?" Cece asked.

"The door was locked with a dead bolt."

"Couldn't the door have been locked with a key from the outside?" Kate asked.

"Yes." Olssen's voice took on an *I'm-in-charge-and-I-know-what-I'm-doing* tone. "But everyone had left the library, and there's no evidence that anyone left after the fire started. Besides, the firemen who investigated it said the fire was definitely started by a cigarette that ignited some papers, so it wasn't arson. They said it was lucky the library was so new and well-built. Even though this room didn't have a sprinkler, it was so locked up it didn't have enough oxygen to allow the fire to get to the outside halls or upstairs. It was pretty well contained here."

He turned and pointed to the ceiling just outside the office door. "If the door had been open, the smoke would have set off the alarm in the hall, and the fire department might have been able to save him." He shook his head. "As it was, the fire was confined to the office, and it was a long time before enough smoke made its way through the cracks to set off the alarm. But by then, it was too late for Mr. Tyme."

"And you don't think there was any foul play involved?" Cece asked with an innocent *I'm-just-a-curious-bystander* expression on her face.

"We didn't find any evidence of anyone else being present. First of all, the other librarian ..." His voice trailed off and he rubbed his chin. "I can't remember her name."

"Miss Culberson?" Cece asked.

"Yes, that's the one. She said she had locked the library as usual when she left. No one could get in without setting off the burglar alarm."

"But somebody could have been hiding inside the library, right?" Kate asked.

"That's right, but they would have set off the burglar alarm when they left the building after the fire. You see, when the alarm in this building is set, it will go off any time a door or window is opened."

"And it didn't go off?" Cece asked.

"No."

"Maybe Mr. Tyme had disarmed the system," Kate said.

"Sorry, Miss Frasier, but the burglar alarm was set. We noted it when we got here."

Kathryn and Cece exchanged a look. "So where does that leave us?" Kate asked.

"Back on square one," Cece responded with a shake of her head.

"Who's on square one?" A young girl's voice breached the conversation and Kate turned to see who was talking.

"Girls, what are you doing here?" Kate asked as Reen and Joanie breezed up.

Reen ignored the question and homed in on Officer Olssen. "Are you a policeman?" she asked.

"Yes, I am." Olssen looked down at the child from his great height. His voice reverberated with an *I'm-your-friendly-policeman* tone. "And what are you two young ladies doing down here? Didn't you see the yellow tape at the top of the stairs? Do you know what that means?"

Reen looked at him with a *who-do-you-think-you're-talking-to* expression on her face. "It means this is a crime scene."

Olssen's mouth fell open, and his soft voice hardened into a *don't-fool-with-me-kid* timbre. "No. That's not what it means," he said. "A dangerous fire took place here, and this area is off limits to the public until all the repairs can be completed. You shouldn't be down here."

Reen ignored him and peeked into the open door. "Is this Mr. Tyme's office?"

Olssen looked in exasperation to Kate. She said, "Officer Olssen, this is Reen Penterson and Joanie Finelson. They think something bad happened to Mr. Tyme and they're trying to find out about it." She shrugged.

Joanie's eyes opened wide. "We think he was murdered."

Olssen gasped. "Girls, you shouldn't be spreading rumors like that. The police have investigated this scene and didn't find any evidence of a crime."

"But it's all very suspicious, isn't it?" Reen squinted at the policeman and rubbed her chin. "We think somebody offed Mr. Tyme and covered it up with a fire."

"And then they locked the office door from the outside and escaped." Joanie bounced up and down on her toes.

Reen tilted her head back to look up at the tall officer. "Not only that. We think Mr. Tyme may have left a clue."

Kate, Olssen, and Cece stared speechless at Reen.

"We read about how Mr. Tyme loved puzzles and mysteries." Reen pointed into the office. "I bet there's a secret compartment somewhere in Mr. Tyme's office where he left a clue to the murderer." She looked up at Officer Olssen. "All we have to do is find it." She took a step toward the office.

Olssen reached out his huge hand and put it on her shoulder. "No. You're not allowed in the office. It's dangerous. As a matter of fact, you're not allowed down here at all." He guided the children toward the stairs at the end of the hallway. "I'm going to escort you upstairs and put you in the custody of Miss Culberson. And don't come back down here."

When they were out of earshot, Cece turned to Kate. "Do you suppose?"

"A secret compartment? That's so Agatha Christie," Kate replied. "That doesn't happen in real life."

When Olssen returned, he found Kate and Cece in the office. Cece was examining the shelves while Kate was running her hand along the edge of the wall next to the window.

Chapter Seventeen

THE RABBI AND THE MINISTER

"Well, that was a losing effort." Kate brushed dirt off her pants as they headed toward the rectory. "Rummaging around a filthy, burned-out office didn't get us anything except dirty clothes."

"Yeah." Cece held one hand in front of her. "And I broke a fingernail trying to pry up one of the floor tiles."

"I didn't think we were going to find anything, but Reen has a way of stirring things up," Kate said. "I'm glad we're out of there and back to trying to decipher the code."

"What did Reverend Whitefield say he wanted to talk about?"

"He said he had found something else he wanted to share with us if we could meet him at the rectory. I told him we were in the library and could walk over right away. There he is, and Rabbi Hart is with him."

Kathryn pointed at two figures strolling along the central path through the quad. One was a short man with a long, gray beard. He was wearing a yarmulke and nodding vigorously as the other, Reverend Whitefield, stooped down to say something.

Rabbi Hart caught sight of them and waved them over. "Ah," he said. "Here are our two favorite detectives!"

"And our two favorite spiritual leaders," Cece said. "You look pretty serious."

"We were talking about the course we're creating for the summer session. The first class is in a couple of weeks," Reverend Whitefield said.

"What's the course?"

"We're biting off a big piece of educational pie," the rabbi said. "Reverend Whitefield and I have created a new course entitled Concepts and Ideas in Judeo-Christian History. The wealth of material is overwhelming, so we're trying to decide how to organize it in a way to make it meaningful."

"Sounds interesting," Kate said. "Why did you decide to teach it?"

The rabbi pulled at his beard. "We live in such a secular society that Reverend Whitefield and I are concerned about the attitude of young people. Many college students come to adulthood without any basis in faith and decide they don't need to examine anything outside their own sensory experience."

"So you're trying to convince the students of a higher power?"

Reverend Whitefield shook his head. "No. We're only interested in presenting facts about history. There's no proselytizing. We simply want the students to examine the history of the Judeo-Christian experience and appreciate the need for humility in the journey of mankind."

"Humility is a pretty underrated virtue in our society," Cece said. "Bellevue U is such a technologically rich university. Why would students want to use part of their time to look inside themselves when they can be learning skills that will be profitable to them?"

"Excellent question." Rabbi Hart motioned with his hand that they should continue their discussion as they walked. "Many people consider the job of mankind to be one of control. They want to build, conquer, rule."

"And you think that's wrong?" Kate asked.

"No," Reverend Whitefield said. "Rabbi Hart and I both believe God commanded mankind to take control of the earth and subdue it." He smiled. "Think of the great inventions throughout history. The printing press made it possible for people to be educated en masse. Automobiles and airplanes enable us to travel great distances safely and in short periods of time. The study of medicine has given us longer, healthier lives. These are all evidence of man conquering his environment."

"Sounds pretty good to me." Cece put her hands on her hips. "I can see why some people would believe in the ability of humankind to solve all our problems."

"But something's missing from this equation," the rabbi said. "While we have made great strides in understanding our environment and using it to make our lives better, we have to remember we are not omnipotent."

"So that's where God comes in?" Kate asked.

A gentle smile spread across Reverend Whitefield's face. "Yes, and that's where the need for humility comes in." They had arrived at the rectory, and he motioned toward the door. "And this is where the second clue comes in."

"The second clue?" Kate felt her eyes open wide. "You found another clue to Mr. Tyme's murder?" Her face grew warm and she glanced at Rabbi Hart. "I mean Mr. Tyme's death."

"Don't worry," the minister said. "I've filled Rabbi Hart in on our suspicions. He's a part of our little group now." He smiled and nodded at the rabbi.

"I'm honored to be one of the team members." Rabbi Hart gave a slight bow.

"I'm glad you're in on it," Cece said. "At least I won't slip up and let the cat out of the bag when I'm at the synagogue one day." She turned back to Reverend Whitefield. "I'm dying to hear. What did you find?"

"Come on in. Jan has some snacks for us."

Chapter Eighteen

THE SILVER CLUE

Jan Whitefield brought out a tray of cookies and tea as they all found seats around the coffee table in the rectory living room.

The reverend disappeared into his study and returned with a book, which he held up for them all to see. "*A Brief History of Time*," he said.

"That's an interesting book to have a clue about Father Time!" Kate said.

"Exactly." Whitefield opened the book. "Mr. Tyme often extolled the brilliance of this work by Stephen Hawking. I think he saw it as a personal journal because of his name. I had asked the police if I could look through Mr. Tyme's apartment after they finished their investigation, and they allowed me to take this book. Knowing Mr. Tyme as I did, I thought he may have left a clue somewhere."

"And?" Cece sat forward on her chair.

Reverend Whitefield opened the book and held it up. Taped to the inside of the cover was a note written on chapel stationery.

> AG - IMPURITY
>
> GOD REMEMBERS

The reverend handed the book to Kate, and she stared at it a moment before reading out loud, "AG - Impurity. What does that mean?"

"I have no idea, but this is a copy of the first prayer request I told you about. Mr. Tyme and I found it last winter, and we wondered what AG was."

"Could it be someone's initials?" Cece asked.

"We thought of that too," Whitefield said, "but we don't have anyone in the congregation with those initials."

"AG sometimes stands for Attorney General." Kathryn tapped on the note. "But somehow I think it's deeper than that."

"Why do you say that, Kathryn?" the rabbi asked.

"It must be some kind of code, maybe related to the Bible." She stood and paced back and forth across the room. "What does AG have to do with impurity?"

"I'm not a scientist," the rabbi said, "but isn't AG a symbol in the periodic table?"

"Yes," Kate said. "It's the code for silver."

"Ah," Reverend Whitefield exclaimed. "I see it now. Do you get it, Mordecai?"

The rabbi's head bobbed up and down. "Yes. Of course. It's a proverb encoded in the prayer request."

Cece raised her eyebrows. "I hope somebody is going to let me in on the secret. What proverb?"

The rabbi bowed toward the minister. "You saw it first, Jim."

Reverend Whitefield bowed in return. "Take away the dross from the silver."

"It's from Proverbs 25:4," the rabbi said. He picked up a Bible from the coffee table, opened it and read, "Take away the dross from the silver, and the smith has material for a vessel."

"AG minus impurity is the same as silver minus dross." Cece shook her head. "Now that's clever, but are you sure that's what it means?"

"No," the minister responded. "But that makes it a proverb encoded at the top, and the phrase God Remembers at the bottom. That's the same pattern we saw in the other prayer request."

Kate stopped pacing and frowned. "But what does this have to do with Mr. Tyme's death?"

"I don't know that either, but the two prayer requests must be related.

You already have a copy of the first one. I made a copy of this one for you, too." Reverend Whitefield handed a separate sheet of paper to Kathryn.

"You said there may have been three prayer requests in all. So we have the first one and the third one," Cece said.

"If he saved the first one," the rabbi said, "he must have saved the second one as well."

"I hope so," Reverend Whitefield said. "I intend to go through some more of Mr. Tyme's things to see if I can find it."

"If that is the proverb about silver, what could the sender be telling us?" Kate asked. "Could it refer to silver artifacts in the church?"

The rabbi leaned forward. "That particular verse is usually interpreted as meaning we need to remove what is bad or foolish in our midst. There are several ways to look at it. For example, a leader must get rid of evil people in his organization."

Kate sat on the arm of one of the wingback chairs. "Could it mean someone was looking at Mr. Tyme as the impurity and killing him was the way to remove it from the organization?"

"That's one way of looking at it," Reverend Whitefield responded. "But I can't think of anyone who saw Mr. Tyme as evil. He was a deacon in the church and reached out to help many people in our community."

"There are other ways of interpreting the proverb," the rabbi said. "It can also be a lesson about humility, meaning someone needs to remove the pride from their behavior."

Jan Whitefield smiled at the group. "That applies to all of us."

"Something's bothering me," Cece said. "You told us that Mr. Tyme burned the prayer requests, but he saved this one."

"Actually, Cece, I think he did burn them, but I believe he copied this particular prayer request before he burned the original. That's why this one is written on chapel stationery." Reverend Whitefield closed the book and tapped the cover.

"From what I understand," the rabbi said, "Mr. Tyme must have suspected something nefarious from the outset and decided to keep a copy of the note."

"Exactly what I was thinking," the reverend said.

"But is that ethical?" Cece asked. "The agreement is that all prayer requests will be burned. Even though he burned the original one, he made a copy."

"That's an important question, Cece, and one we can't ignore." Reverend Whitefield stared down at the book. "I have an obligation to abide by the rules of this church."

Rabbi Hart pulled on his beard. "In Jewish thought, there may be an exception to such a rule."

They all turned to him.

"How can there be an exception?" Kate asked. "The rule is clear, and it's designed to protect the people in the church. If someone found out Mr. Tyme wasn't burning the prayer requests, they might lose confidence in the honesty of the church." She faced the minister. "And the clergy."

"That's true, Kathryn," the rabbi replied. "However, one must weigh the consequences of two courses of action. If Mr. Tyme feared a serious crime had been committed, he would be remiss if he didn't follow up. As long as he didn't use his knowledge to damage someone in the church community, and it's obvious he took great pains to conceal his actions, then he may have done a great service."

"This is where things get murky for me," Kathryn said. "I want everything to be black or white. When we get into the gray area, I feel uncomfortable." She smiled at the rabbi. "Maybe I should enroll in the course you two are teaching."

"I know what you mean about things being murky, Kathryn," Reverend Whitefield said. "Sometimes we don't know what the best course of action is. Yes, Mr. Tyme obeyed the letter of the law by burning the original request, but did he obey the spirit of it?"

He looked around the room. "Including Jan, there are now five of us who know the contents of two of the three prayer requests. It's critical that we keep the specifics to ourselves, but we owe it to Mr. Tyme to try to discover the secrets hidden in them. I feel an obligation to hold onto these because I think they may be relevant to Mr. Tyme's death." He held the book up. "I hope you'll be able to decipher the code soon. Maybe that will lead us to a better understanding of what Mr. Tyme was up to."

Chapter Nineteen

DINNERTIME

My dad calls himself a creature of habit. That means he always does things the same way. Take, for example, our dinnertime routine. Dad comes home from work and Mrs. Toussaint has dinner all prepared. She likes my dad, so she always cooks his favorite meals and puts everything on the table right at seven o'clock. Then she tells me to wash my hands, and she fusses around like one of the hens we saw at the farm we visited last year.

Our dinners are like little programs. First, Dad says the food is delicious. Then he says, "Doris, I don't know how you do it. Every meal is better than the one before." I think this is a little overkill, but Mrs. Toussaint loves it. She always says, "Nate, I know you're just being nice, but I appreciate it."

And then he says "No, Doris. I really mean it." He takes another couple of bites and does a long "mmmm" just to add emphasis, then he turns to me.

"And how is Miss Irene? What new things did you do today?" When my dad and I are alone, his voice is always gentle, but at dinner he acts perky. I think it's just for Mrs. Toussaint's sake.

I tell him about my day. If nothing interesting happened, I make something up. He always wants to know if I fell down or scraped my knees again, and sometimes he grins and pinches my arm, and it makes me feel important.

Tonight, we went through the usual routine. I decided not to mention my investigation into Mr. Tyme's death, so I told him about the bell tower instead. He looked happy and said he was glad Joanie and I were using our time wisely. I smiled and tried to look obedient.

Mrs. Toussaint stood up and said, "Time for dishes!" That's code for me to take the dishes off the table and load the dishwasher. It's my chore. Dad goes to his study and Mrs. Toussaint tidies up. Then she peeks into his office to say goodnight. There's a lot of that "Thank you again, you're wonderful" stuff, and then she leaves and goes to the guesthouse out back.

Eight o'clock is my favorite time of day. That's the time I go to Dad's study, and he usually says, "Come in, my dear" in a funny accent. And then he adds, "What's your pleasure? A game? A book?"

I can tell he wants our time to be a learning experience. If we play Scrabble, he usually lets me win so I'll get good at words. "Reen, you clobbered me! We're going to have to find another game so I can win." Or sometimes I sit next to him on the couch, and he reads to me even though I'm a good reader. Other times, we play a Proverbs game he made up with cards or he takes the Bible down and asks me to read to him.

But my very favorite is when he says he wants to talk and he tells me about what it's like to be a professor, or he asks what I'm thinking about doing when I grow up, or we talk about grown-up things like friendship and doing good deeds. That's when I feel my heart smiling, and I don't want our special time together to end.

* * *

Nate pushed his laptop aside and rubbed his eyes. He had managed to clean out his inbox and he checked his watch. Eight o'clock on the dot.

Reen bounded into his office with a game box under her arm. She plopped down in the chair opposite his desk and put the box on her lap.

"Okay. What torture do you have in store for me tonight?" Nate grinned at her.

"It's Big Boggle. You're better than I am, so you'll win."

"I doubt it." He pushed some papers out of the way and cleared a space on the desk. "But first," he said and held up his index finger. "Today is Wednesday, so we should play the Proverbs game."

He reached in his desk drawer and pulled out a deck of cards. They had the words "Proverbs for Irene" on the backs. Nate shuffled the cards and fanned them out like a magician. He held them out to Reen. "Pick a proverb, m'lady."

Reen looked at the deck and carefully chose one from the middle. She handed it to him without looking at it.

Nate turned the card over so only he could see the verse and read it. "Good one," he said. "Proverbs 16 verse 3."

Reen thought a minute, then she grinned. "Commit your work to the Lord, and your plans will be established."

"Excellent!" Nate pushed the card back in the deck and wrapped the rubber band around it. "You're getting so good at these, I'm going to have to make another deck that's harder."

Reen smiled and swung her legs back and forth. "It's fun. I'm good at memorizing."

"Yes, you are. But the proverbs are for more than just memorizing, right? They're for us to know how to behave in life. My father played this game with me when I was a boy."

"But your father was a minister. It was his job to make you learn the Bible. You're a college professor. Why do I have to learn the proverbs?"

"It's every parent's job to give his child guidance." He dropped the deck of cards back into his desk drawer. "And I can't think of a better place to get guidance than from the Bible."

"I know." She had stopped listening and was opening the game box. "But playing Big Boggle is more fun."

By nine o'clock, Reen had identified many more words than Nate. "I give up," he said. "You're getting so good at this game, I'm going to have to stop playing." He looked down at his watch. "Besides, it's about time for me to get back to work."

Reen gathered up the pieces and threw them in the box. She gave him a cagey smile. "I know you're letting me win, Dad."

He placed his laptop back in the center of the desk and smiled over at her. "I don't let you win. I just make a few unforced errors now and then."

She grinned at him. "That's nice of you." Then she skipped around the desk and hugged him. "Good night, Dad."

"Good night to you, my wonderful daughter. I'll be there in a few minutes to tuck you in."

"Okay, Dad." Reen looked up at him with an expression of eager anticipation on her face. "Dad, about that proverb we read tonight."

"What is it, honey?"

"Should I always do what I think is right?" She tilted her head and opened her eyes wide.

"Yes, honey. We should always do what we think is right."

A big smile spread across her face. "That's what I thought." She grabbed the box and headed out the door.

For several seconds, Nate looked at the door his daughter had just closed behind her. Then he picked up the picture of his late wife from his desk and held it in front of him. "She's doing well, Trish. You'd be so proud of your little girl. She's just like you. Smart and capable, and she says she always wants to do what's right." He put the picture down and said out loud, "So why do I get the feeling she's up to something?"

Chapter Twenty

THE CRYPTOGRAPHY EXHIBIT

Joanie usually skips when we walk across campus. She's a good skipper. But today she just trudged along beside me. She didn't even smile at Mrs. Toussaint when we said goodbye to her. And I know why.

The only reason Joanie ever turns glum and moody is because of her father. When she drags her feet like she was doing today, it means Uncle Jayce came to her house last night and had a fight with her mom.

Uncle Jayce left them a year ago, and it makes Joanie sad. She keeps telling me she wants him to come home. She thinks he doesn't love her, or he wouldn't have left. When I told her once she should forget about her dad, she cried, so I don't say that anymore.

I told my dad I hated Joanie's father, and I called him "Uncle Jayce the Jerk." Dad said I should never say that again. It would upset Joanie and besides, he said, "Things will probably turn out all right in the long run. Uncle Jayce just has some issues to work out."

Issues? I have issues! My last year's teacher, Mrs. Tuddle, told me I'm not living up to my potential and I should study harder. And she said she's going to talk to my next year's teacher, Mr. Wittson, so he'll know all about me. Uncle Jayce doesn't have to worry about teachers.

I was trying to figure out what to do about Joanie when I saw Kathryn Frasier walking toward the computer science building. Joanie likes

Kathryn a lot, so I figured if we could tag along with her, it would get Joanie out of the doldrums.

"Hi, Kathryn," I shouted out and waved.

"Hello, Reen. Hi, Joanie." She walked over to us. "How's your elbow, Reen?" Kathryn leaned down and looked at my skinned-up arm. She touched the Band-Aid real gently like she was afraid she might hurt me.

I shrugged. "It's okay. Where are you going?"

"I'm going to see the cryptography exhibit."

"What's that?" Joanie asked.

"It's an exhibit all about secret codes and things like that. The computer science department is displaying it in the lobby of their building." She started to move away.

I grabbed her hand before she could get very far. "Can we go with you? Maybe we could learn something."

Kathryn looked like she wasn't sure this was such a good idea.

"Please," Joanie said. That did it.

"Okay. You can come, but you have to be quiet."

Joanie took Kathryn's hand and skipped toward the building.

The front hall in the computer science building is usually a pretty boring place. Just a bunch of pictures of old guys standing around old machines that nobody would use today. They even have a card punch and some kind of ancient typewriter. But when we walked in, the hall looked like an exhibit at the kids' tech museum in Denver. Cool.

Kathryn said she saw some friends she wanted to talk to, so Joanie and I wandered around the room by ourselves. One wall had a display of all kinds of puzzles. My favorite showed word anagrams where you had to figure out a word by moving the letters around.

Joanie saw a sign labeled Memory Devices and dragged me over to read it. There was a big picture of all the planets in the solar system. Underneath the picture it said, "My Very Educated Mother Just Served Us Noodles."

"Look," she said. "It's called mnemonics. You can remember the names of the planets in order from the sun by the first letter in each word.

Mercury, Venus, Earth, Mars, Jupiter, Saturn, Uranus, and Neptune." Joanie's really into things like that.

I said we should make up some of our own mnemonics so we'd be like spies.

"Joan Penterson Finelson," she said and giggled. "Just plain fantastic."

"Irene Elizabeth Penterson," I said. "Intelligent private eye."

"That's not fair," Joanie said. "You switched the letters around." Joanie always likes to play by the rules.

"I anagrammed my mnemonic," I said and gave her a big thumbs-up. "Hey, I have an idea." I took my phone out of my pocket.

We took pictures of the displays on the wall and then we started taking pictures of everything else in the room. It got to be a game. We pretended like we were spies and got pictures of everybody. One guy scowled at me like I was a pest, so I told him I was doing a project for school. He just turned his back and walked away.

After thirty minutes or so, things got boring. We'd played all the games, so we looked for Kathryn.

I spotted her standing by a glass case, talking to a guy with a rumpled shirt that matched his messy hair. Definitely a computer science kind of guy. Mrs. Toussaint calls them gerds. I think she means geeks or nerds, but she gets them mixed up. She says university people might be smart, but most of them just sit around mumbling into their ties. I'm not sure what that means. My father hardly ever wears a tie.

There were a couple of other guys loitering around Kathryn. I bet her boyfriend wouldn't like that. I recognized Andrew Bellinger. He's in my dad's department and he came to our house once when Dad invited the faculty over.

We sauntered over, and I heard Rumple Guy say, "That's not my area. Andrew is the expert on codes and ciphers." I touched Kathryn's sleeve.

"Oh, hi girls." She smiled. "Did you get some good pictures?"

"Lots," I said, and I looked directly at Rumple Guy. That's the way you get adults to introduce you.

"This is my friend Tommy. Tommy, this is Reen." She put her hand on my shoulder and gestured toward Joanie. "And this is Joanie."

Tommy looked to be about as shy as Joanie is. I could tell by the way he kept pulling at his ear, like he wasn't sure what to do with his hands. But his face was kind. He looked like the type who would escort a spider out of his house rather than step on it. I like people like that. They're usually easy to get information out of.

Tommy said "hi," and Andrew Bellinger yawned. I thought Tommy looked promising, like the type who knows a lot and might spill the beans, so I came right out with it. "We're writing a paper on university buildings. What do you know about the fire in the library?"

Tommy's mouth fell open, and Andrew just turned around and walked away. I guess he wasn't going to stick around to talk to kids.

I was about to ask Tommy more about the library when there was a noise by the front door. The first thing I saw was a bright red-and-orange scarf wrapped around the neck of one of the strangest people I ever saw. Finally, things were getting interesting.

Chapter Twenty-One

ROSE RAMEN TAKES THE STAGE

"Who is that?" Tommy asked.

Another visitor to the cryptography exhibit chimed in. "You mean what is that?"

Kate turned and saw a woman with flyaway gray hair entering the room. She wore a multicolored, mid-calf shapeless dress and a bright red-and-orange scarf coiled around her neck. Her glasses were large and rose-tinted with heavy black plastic frames, and her earrings were long and swingy with red and purple beads. She leaned on a black cane with a silver lion's head on top. She stopped just inside the room and peered around as if having difficulty seeing everyone. Voices in the room dropped like the sudden end of a rainstorm.

"Is Kathryn Frasier in attendance?" she asked in a hoarse voice.

Kate timidly raised her hand.

The woman pointed her cane directly at Kathryn. "Ah. There you are." She marched over in black orthopedic shoes, and the assembled guests parted like the Red Sea opening up for Moses. She drew herself up to a rather diminutive height in front of Kate. "Kathryn Frasier, is it?"

"Yes."

"I'm Rose Ramen." She held out a wrinkled and age-spotted hand. "I'm so glad to have the chance to finally meet you in person." She grabbed

Kate's hand and shook it vigorously. "I called your home and your sister told me I could find you here."

Kate pressed her lips together to stifle the laugh that was trying to make its way out. "I'm so glad to meet you, Mrs. Ramen."

"It's Miss Ramen, dear. *Miss* Ramen."

"Oh, I see. And I'm glad you had a chance to talk to my sister, Cece. I wish she were here."

"Ah, yes. Cece Goldman. What an interesting name. I'll have to use it in a book someday." The old woman waved her cane around and some of the people who had drawn close to hear the conversation ducked back out of the way. "I take it you're researching the topic of codes for me here?"

"Yes, I am." Kathryn was beginning to believe this really was a woman named Rose Ramen. "This is Tommy Abrahams. He and Andrew Bellinger were helping me understand various kinds of ciphers."

Rose adjusted her glasses and leaned toward Tommy. "Excellent. Do you know much about secret codes? I'm writing a mystery novel and I want to include several encrypted messages. Kathryn is helping me."

"It's nice to meet you, Ms. Ramen." Tommy made a slight bow. "Andrew is the real expert on codes, but he seems to have left." He shook hands with her. "I've never met a real mystery author before. What's the name of your book?"

Rose squinted her green eyes at him and nodded slowly. "That's a great question. I haven't decided on the title yet. I think maybe I'll have to wait until I get all the codes worked out." She pulled a handkerchief out from under her sleeve and gently dabbed at her nose.

Tommy raised an eyebrow. "Don't authors always have a working title for their books?"

"Yes. That's right. I just don't want anybody else to hear it." She looked furtively around the room and lowered her voice to just above a whisper. "It's all very hush-hush, you see. The name of my book is ..." She looked down at the exhibit case that held a treasure map. "It's called *Murder in the Map Room*."

"Exciting," Tommy said. "Can you tell us the general arc of the plot?"

"Uh uh," she said and waggled her index finger at him. "No hints. I want my book to explode onto the literary scene as a complete surprise!" She spread her fingers and made a wide arc with her hand. "That way I'll make it to all the bestseller lists."

Chapter Twenty-Two

ANDREW BELLINGER

Kate found an empty bench on the edge of the quad. She looked up at the trees all around, wondering if Reen was hiding out again, but there was no one there.

Cece had been a hit at the cryptography exhibit. Reen and Joanie had latched on to Rose Ramen and peppered her with questions about her book. Cece had actually managed to convince them to go home and write a mystery story. Then she had waltzed out of the exhibit and left campus.

But Kathryn hadn't gotten any more information. Tommy said cryptography wasn't his area of expertise but had introduced her to Andrew Bellinger. He was supposed to be an expert, but he had disappeared before she had a chance to talk to him. Maybe she could call his office later.

She sat and took out a notepad. She had memorized the twenty-eight letters of the coal code and she jotted them down at the top of the page. But she had run out of ways to solve it. Everything she tried just returned a jumble of letters. *Maybe it isn't letters. Maybe it's a series of numbers.* She closed her eyes and tried to imagine how to decode a string of letters that represented numbers.

"Don't you work?" A male voice sliced into her silence.

Kate jumped and opened her eyes. A man stood in front of her, but with the sun behind him, she couldn't see who it was. She shaded her eyes as he settled onto the bench beside her. It was Andrew Bellinger.

"I see you here all the time. Don't you have a job?" he said.

"Oh, hi, Andrew." She smiled at him. "I'm a software developer and I can work flexible hours because I work remotely. I've been on campus a lot to meet my sister, Cece, so we can have lunch together."

"What's this?" He pointed to the notepad. "Writing secret messages?"

Kate felt her face get warm. *Did he see the code?* She flipped the notepaper over to a clean sheet. "Just trying to come up with some interesting codes for Miss Ramen's novel."

"I saw that strange woman when she came into the exhibit. You're really going to create some secret codes for her book?"

"Sure," Kate said. "Why not?"

"Maybe I can help." He reached over and took the notepad from her.

Kate held her breath as he took a pen out of his pocket, but he didn't turn back to the page with the code.

"You can have a simple substitution code like this." He wrote the alphabet at the top of the page, then another alphabet under it that was three letters off.

```
ABCDEFGHIJKLMNOPQRSTUVWXYZ
xyzabcdefghijklmnopqrstuvw
```

"Let's say you want to encode the message 'Have a nice day.' All you do is substitute the letters in the second line for the ones in the first line." He wrote the encoded message.

```
exsbxkfzbaxv
```

"To decipher it, just do the reverse operation." He wrote the decoded message underneath.

```
exsbxkfzbaxv
HAVEANICEDAY
```

"These are trivial to break."

Kate nodded. "Yes. I've seen those before. But Miss Ramen says she wants a code that's really complicated."

"In that case, let's try the two-directional cipher where we alternate letters from the beginning and end of the alphabet as the key. I'll start the offset four letters in." He jotted down the alphabet again but this time he alternated letters from the beginning and end of the alphabet in the second line.

```
ABCDEFGHIJKLMNOPQRSTUVWXYZ
lomnazbycxdwevfugthsirjqkp
```

He wrote a coded message underneath.

```
ylrancvvatjcsyea
```

"You can decode it by reversing the process."

"Are you going to decode it for me?" Kate asked.

"Why don't you decode it yourself?" He gave her the pen and waited as she deciphered each letter.

```
ylrancvvatjcsyea
HAVEDINNERWITHME
```

She looked up at him and smiled. "That's very cute."

He leaned back and spread his arms across the back of the bench. "How about it? Do you feel like having dinner with me tonight at the Franklin Cafe?"

Kate blushed. "I would like to, Andrew, but I'm in a relationship with someone and we've decided not to see other people."

"Ah." He frowned and removed his arms from the bench. "The good ones are all taken. Either they're married or they're in a serious relationship."

Just at that moment, the clock on the bell tower struck one. Kate took advantage of it to change the subject. "I love that clock," she said. "Did you know Mr. Tyme was in charge of the maintenance of it? He was a wonderful man. It's a shame what happened to him."

"I don't have any use for the bell tower clock," Andrew said. "I have a perfectly good watch, and I know how to read time." He stood abruptly. "Good luck with your codes. If you want to get really sophisticated, you might talk to Isabelle Cassidy. She was a professor here before she retired. Rumor has it she works with the NSA. Cipher expert." He turned and strode quickly away.

* * *

Andrew felt a drop of sweat slide down the side of his face, and he wiped it away with the back of his hand.

Why had Kathryn Frasier been so quick to bring up Mr. Tyme's name? Did she know something?

He took a deep breath as he grabbed the door to the computer science building and yanked it open.

Forget it. She can't possibly know anything.

Chapter Twenty-Three

ISABELLE CASSIDY

"Remind me who this is." Cece followed Kate along the sidewalk by the small ranch-style brick house just outside the campus.

"It's Isabelle Cassidy. Dr. Isabelle Cassidy. Andrew Bellinger told me about her, and I checked with Tommy. She used to be in the Computer Science Department, but Tommy said she retired a couple of years ago. He said she's an expert on codes. He thinks she worked secretly for the NSA, deciphering messages from foreign governments."

"The NSA? Like in spies and Interpol and danger?" Cece stopped. "All of a sudden I don't feel so good. Maybe I should wait in the car."

Kate looked back at her sister. "Don't pull that one. We both agreed to figure this out."

Cece started walking again. "How do we know she's not the killer? I mean, if she worked for the NSA, she's probably Wonder Woman in disguise. We could be putting the enemy on the team."

"Tommy said she was on sabbatical in Washington, DC, for the last year. She just got back a couple of weeks ago. That would have been after Mr. Tyme died." She stepped up onto the small porch. "Besides, I asked Reverend Whitefield about her, and he said he knows her. He says there's no way she could have killed Mr. Tyme."

"How does he know that?"

"He said we'd understand when we meet her." Kate rang the doorbell. "Courage, big sister. Courage."

A young woman opened the door and motioned them into the room. "Hi. I'm Sissy. I'm a student in the medical school and I help Dr. Cassidy out at home. Come on in. She's expecting you." She led them back through a living area into a broad sunroom. In the middle of the room, a woman sat in a wheelchair with a large book on her lap. Kathryn remembered seeing her at the cryptography exhibit. She had been sitting off to the side with a group of people around her as if she was special.

She had a prominent nose over a mouth that was full and wide. Her gray hair was cropped short and brushed back away from her face. She wore a white blouse with black slacks and black flats.

Kate was drawn to her eyes. Even from where she stood, she could see the dark blue rim around the blue-green irises. The woman stared at her with a laser-like expression softened by a hint of humor in the tiny smile that lifted the corners of her lips.

"Dr. Cassidy?"

"Yes. I'm Isabelle Cassidy." Her voice had a whispery quality. Before Kate could introduce herself, the woman said, "And you're Kathryn Frasier. It's good to meet you." She held out her hand, and Kate felt her own hand enveloped in the woman's iron grip. Her eyes held Kate's.

"I knew your father when he was here at the university," Dr. Cassidy said. "I was sorry to hear of his accident. He was a wonderful colleague."

"Thank you, Dr. Cassidy. My father loved his time here as a professor." Kate dropped her hand and gestured toward Cece. "This is my sister, Cece Goldman. She's helping me with my project."

Dr. Cassidy trained her eyes on Cece. Her smile turned into a wry grin. "Cece Goldman. That author lady at the cryptography exhibit said she had talked to you on the phone. Let's see. What was her name?" She paused and snapped her fingers. "Oh yes. It was Rose Ramen. Too bad you weren't there to see her in person."

Kathryn caught the slight inflection in Dr. Cassidy's voice and wondered what it could mean. Cece looked a little uncomfortable.

Cece held out her hand. "It's nice to meet you, Dr. Cassidy."

Dr. Cassidy ignored the offer of a handshake and reached for Cece's left hand instead. "What a lovely watch." She leaned forward to examine it more closely. "It looks unique. I especially like the little chain designed to protect the watch from falling off." She continued to hold Cece's hand. "You should take good care of such a beautiful piece of jewelry, Cece." She smiled up at her. "Or should I say Rose?"

Cece's mouth dropped open and she stuttered, "I ... I don't know what you mean."

Dr. Cassidy's laugh was light but hearty. "It was an excellent disguise, but you made one small mistake."

Kate and Cece looked at each other in wonder. There was nothing to do but admit it.

"How did you know?"

"I didn't know until you walked in just now." She let go of Cece's hand. "It was the watch. You should never wear your personal jewelry when you're trying to deceive people."

Cece looked down at her wrist. "But I had tucked my watch under the sleeve of my outfit."

"Not completely. At the exhibit, I noticed the little gold chain peeking out. That's a kind of watch you rarely see anymore. It's somewhat old-fashioned, perfect for Rose Ramen, but it doesn't seem to fit the current styles of young women today." She nodded toward Cece's hand. "The truth is always in the details."

Cece blushed crimson. "You're the first person who's ever uncovered my real identity after I've gone in disguise. I'm impressed."

Dr. Cassidy motioned for them to sit down. "I've made a career of uncovering things in disguise. Yours was quite good. I don't believe anyone else would have known." She turned back to Kate. "I'm assuming you two are up to some subterfuge, and you're here to seek my help."

Kate settled herself on the couch. "Dr. Cassidy, I'm amazed. Do you also know what we're looking into?"

Dr. Cassidy laughed again. "No. Sorry. I'm only observant, not prescient. Why don't you tell me what's going on?"

Kathryn relaxed. "We've been asked to look into the death of Mr. Tyme. Someone thinks there may be something suspicious about it, and they suggested you might help us."

"I knew Mr. Tyme, and I heard he had died, but the information I received was that it was an accidental fire."

"That was the official report. But there was a note left in the prayer box at the university chapel. It may have a clue to Mr. Tyme's death."

"Ah. I'm guessing there is some kind of code involved, and someone told you I worked in the field."

"Exactly. They say you're an expert, and that's certainly what we need." She pulled the copy of the prayer request out of her purse and handed it over.

Dr. Cassidy looked at it intently. "Is this the actual paper that was left in the box, or is it a copy?"

"It's a copy. Normally they burn the prayer requests after they've been read and prayed over, but Reverend Whitefield says he saved this one since it could have to do with a crime. He has the original."

Dr. Cassidy looked again at the paper and muttered, "A time to live and a time to die. The writer apparently took some liberty with the Scripture. He or she didn't quote it precisely. That's your first clue."

"Why is that a clue? Does it mean the writer doesn't know much about the Bible?"

"I suspect it's the exact opposite. Let's assume it's a man. If he didn't know the Scripture, he'd look it up and copy it exactly. However, if he knows it well, he may just paraphrase the part that's germane." She read it again. "You're assuming 'a time to live and a time to die' refers to Mr. Tyme's death?"

"Yes. Doesn't it seem like someone taking credit for the murder? Sort of like doing a victory lap?"

"Interesting thought. Of course, it could be someone who was glad to see Mr. Tyme die. Or maybe it isn't about Mr. Tyme at all. Maybe it just happened to be left at around the same time." She squinted at the paper. "Coals on his head." She looked up at Kate. "You think it refers to the fire?"

"Yes."

Dr. Cassidy continued down the page. "God remembers. What do you think that means?"

"Whoever left this could have a grudge against Mr. Tyme. Maybe some perceived injustice from the past."

"Hmm. And the letters on the third line. That's what you want my help with?"

"Yes. I haven't been able to get anywhere with the code. I tried simple substitution ciphers, but it's beyond my capabilities. I thought you might give me some guidance." Kate decided not to mention the other prayer requests. If Dr. Cassidy could help her with this one code, she wouldn't have to know about the others.

Chapter Twenty-Four

HOW SMART PEOPLE WALK

"Look. There's Andrew Bellinger." I was sitting on the lowest limb of an old magnolia tree, swinging my legs and practicing my balance. "Remember, we saw him at the cryptography exhibit a few days ago."

Joanie was sitting on the ground, leaning against the trunk. "I didn't like him. He frowned at me." She looked around. "Where is he?"

"There." I pointed to him as he walked through the quad. "He's very smart."

"How do you know he's smart?"

"I heard Tommy say he was an expert on something. You have to be smart to be an expert. Besides, you can tell how smart he is by the way he walks." I jumped down and put my hands behind my back and imitated him. "See. He goes up on his toes with every step." I took a few steps and Joanie giggled.

"You'd think he'd run into something the way he's looking at his feet and not where he's going," she said.

I watched him for another few seconds. "He's probably counting his steps or measuring his stride. That's the kind of thing smart people do."

"Remember how Mrs. Toussaint told us we should practice walking with a book on our heads to be poised?" Joanie stood beside me. She put her hand on top of her head and walked real slow, pretending she was trying to keep it from falling off.

"I don't think Mrs. Toussaint knows much about smart people." I flipped my thumb toward Andrew. "Nerdy people walk like that. They probably learned it in grad school. Maybe it makes their brains work faster." I picked a dandelion and blew the fluffs off. "I wonder if he knows anything about Mr. Tyme."

Andrew ran up the stairs to the library, taking them two at a time, like he was in a hurry. I never saw anybody look like they really wanted to go into the library. Most of the students just sit around on the steps looking bored.

"C'mon," I said. "Let's follow him." I grabbed Joanie's hand and pulled her up.

"What are you going to say to him?" Joanie trotted next to me as we headed to the library.

"I'm going to ask if he was around when the fire happened and then question him about it. I'll tell him it's for a paper we're writing for school."

"Suppose he knows you're not telling the truth?"

I stopped and gave her a look. "Adults never question you when you say you're doing something for school." We started up again.

Actually, Andrew seemed pretty cool, like the kind of person who could help us. And he was young enough so he wouldn't be stuffy about everything. He might even want to get in on the ground floor of our investigation. We could take him to the office where Mr. Tyme was killed, and he could help us figure out what happened. Smart people are good at that.

* * *

Miss Culberson was stacking books when we came in. She wasn't as friendly after I told her we were investigating Mr. Tyme's death, but we tried to be nice so she wouldn't think we were suspicious of her. She put her index finger to her lips. "Don't forget, girls. We have to be quiet in the library."

While Joanie smiled at her, I saw Andrew going up the stairs to the second level. I gave Joanie a head motion that meant we should follow him.

By the time we got to the top of the stairs, I had lost him. I pointed to the back half of the floor and whispered to Joanie, "You go to Fiction. I'll cover Biographies."

Joanie headed toward Fiction while I turned to the stacks at the left. I started at Adams and went really fast until I saw a book about Sally Ride. I stopped to look at it.

I was leafing through all the pictures of the space shuttle crew when Joanie came around the corner and scampered up to me with her finger on her lips. "Shh."

I figured she was doing an imitation of Miss Culberson. I shrugged and mouthed the word "What?"

Joanie's eyes got wide and round, like moons, and her eyebrows practically jumped off her head. She pointed toward the fiction section and made little kissy motions with her lips. Then she started to giggle. She put both hands over her mouth so she wouldn't make any noise, but she couldn't stop laughing.

I whispered, "Somebody's kissing?" I felt my eyebrows take off to parts unknown.

Joanie nodded her head up and down while she continued to hold her hands over her mouth. Whatever it was must be good. "Show me," I whispered.

Joanie did this exaggerated tiptoe thing back toward Fiction. She looked like a cartoon of the blue heron I see at the park that picks his foot up out of the water and takes a really slo-o-o-w step forward before he puts it carefully back in. I think he's trying to sneak up on the fish, but I never saw him catch one. I gave Joanie a little shove on her shoulder and waved my hand so she'd hurry up. A good reporter knows you have to move fast when the opportunity presents itself.

We were almost to the end of the fiction stacks when Joanie stopped and pointed. Whoever it was, they were against the wall in the last row of We—Z. We crept real quietly into the Tr—Wa row. As we passed Anthony Trollope, I saw an opening ahead at Mark Twain. I tiptoed up to it. There was a space next to *The Adventures of Tom Sawyer.*

A guy and a girl were standing on the other side of the stack, and they were all wrapped around each other, making soft noises. I couldn't see their faces, but she had glossy black hair that hung halfway down her back.

The guy mumbled something like "honey," but I couldn't hear much because he was talking so low. He was hugging and kissing her. When he pulled his head back, I almost gasped out loud. It was Andrew. He pushed the girl against the wall.

Joanie tugged on my sleeve because she wanted to see too, but the space was too small for both of us. I waved her away and leaned in to try to hear.

The girl pushed Andrew away and said, "No. Not here." This was like watching a movie my father wouldn't let me see.

He was still trying to kiss her. "C'mon, baby. You know you want this."

She got a little louder and pushed him again. "No."

He stood back and stared at her. "What's the matter, babe? You can't make it with a mere professor?"

Joanie tugged at my sleeve again, and I frowned at her to make her stop. She threw up her hands like she was getting mad because she couldn't see anything. Andrew was talking and saying something like, "What? I'm not as good as silver?" Silver? What did that mean? Joanie kept pulling on my shirt, and I knew I had to do something before she made a fuss and gave us away.

There was this big, giant book next to *Tom Sawyer*. If I could get it out, we could both see the show. I gently pulled it. I tried to move it so it didn't make any sound, but it was really heavy. When I eased it over the edge of the shelf, it started to fall and I couldn't catch it. There was a giant crash when it hit the floor.

I tried to duck, but Andrew turned around so fast he saw me. He glared at me like he could nail me to the spot with his eyes.

"What are you doing over there?" he shouted and started to move around the end of the aisle to where Joanie and I were.

I grabbed Joanie's hand and pulled her toward the stairs. She tripped and fell over the book and dropped my hand.

Andrew was rushing up the aisle looking like a bull who wanted to gore us.

"Quick," I yelled at Joanie. She jumped up and caught my hand again, and we raced down the stairs. I never saw Joanie move that fast before. She even got ahead of me.

Miss Culberson looked up from her desk as we flew by. "Now girls, don't run," she said.

Chapter Twenty-Five

SILVER

Kate felt the effects of the ten-miler she had run that morning as she walked through the quad on the way to the drama building. She stopped to lean against a bench and stretch her calf muscles. The campus was peaceful and quiet, with no one else in sight.

"Help! Kathryn, help!" She heard Reen's voice before she saw the two girls running toward her. They were holding hands and looked terrified. They rushed up to her so fast, Reen almost knocked her over.

"Girls." Kate caught Reen by the shoulders. "What's wrong?"

"It's Andrew," Reen wheezed out as she gasped to catch her breath. "He's after us." She looked back toward the library.

"Andrew?" Kate looked in the direction Reen was pointing.

"Andrew Bellinger. You remember. From the cryptography exhibit. He got mad at us and now he's chasing us."

Joanie's face was scarlet red from running. She looked all around as if making sure there was no one there. She turned back and looked up at Kate. "We saw him kissing a girl in the library. It was shocking," she said in a high, breathless voice.

Kate tried not to smile. She led the girls to the bench and made them sit down. "There's nothing wrong with Andrew kissing a girl."

"But you're not supposed to kiss in the library," Joanie said.

Reen rolled her eyes. "It's not that, Joanie." She refocused on Kate. "He was kissing her and she told him to stop and then he saw us."

Joanie grabbed Kate's hand. "And then he chased us. I think he was going to beat us up."

Kate looked around. "Well, I think he gave up the chase." She squeezed Joanie's hand. "I guess you're too fast for him. Maybe he just wanted to scare you."

"He looked really mean when he was talking to that girl. His face got all red." Reen looked over her shoulder again.

Kate frowned. "What else did he say?"

Joanie's grip loosened and she tilted her head to the side. "Um. He said he wasn't important like silver."

"Silver?" Kate stood up straight. The hair on the back of her neck tingled. "What did he say about silver?"

"That's all," Reen said. "He just told her he wasn't like silver."

"Silver was a horse," Joanie said and giggled. "I know it was the Lone Ranger's horse because Sammy Woods gave a report on it in school."

Reen's eyes half closed. "Why would he say he wasn't like a horse?"

Kathryn leaned down. "Try to remember exactly what he said about silver."

Joanie put her chin in her hands. "I think he said he wasn't as important as silver and he was just a mere professor, or something like that." She looked at Reen.

Reen shrugged. "That's all I remember."

Why would Andrew be talking about silver? Kate looked around, but saw no one else on the quad. "All right, girls," she said. "I'll walk you back to Reen's house, and I suggest you stay out of the library for a while."

* * *

Kate waited for Dr. Penterson. Reen and Joanie had been breathlessly telling Mrs. Toussaint all about Andrew chasing them out of the library until Mrs. Toussaint looked half-hysterical and called Dr. Penterson. Kate had stayed until he arrived home and had a chance to talk to the girls.

"No need for you to stay. I'm sure it's just a case of a young man trying to scare off some little girls who saw more than they were supposed to see. Andrew Bellinger is an associate professor in my department. He's got a pretty short fuse, but there's no way he's going to harm the girls." He walked Kate out to the sidewalk. "Thanks for bringing them home, though. Maybe this will cure them from snooping around."

Kate smiled up at him. "Reen seems like a very curious child. I doubt you can stop her from snooping just because one faculty member got a little sore."

"Yes, you're right about Reen. It's hard to refocus her attention once she sets her mind on something, but I need to find another activity she can get involved in."

"I got interested in running when I was about Reen's age," Kate said. "There's a program called Bellevue Kids Run that you could check into. Reen is an athletic child, and she might like it."

"Thanks. I'll keep that in mind. In the meantime, I'll have a talk with both of them tonight. Again. And I'll give Andrew a call. Thanks for helping out, and you be careful going home."

Kate crossed the street and walked along the sidewalk toward the campus parking lot where she had left her car. The sun had set and the few streetlights laid eerie shadows along the dark street. As she passed a hedge of bushes, Kate heard a rustling sound. She stopped and turned to look. Seeing nothing, she moved ahead. After a few steps, she thought she heard a scraping sound on the sidewalk behind her, as if someone was pulling something along the sidewalk. She whirled around. Still nothing.

Her heartbeat picked up a notch, and her breath quickened. She took two quick steps and turned again. She saw the bushes move several yards behind her. She pulled her keys out of her handbag and sprinted the hundred yards to the parking lot.

When she got to her car, she fumbled with the remote, trying to find the unlock button. She punched it, heard the beep, and jerked the car door open. She practically dove into the driver's seat, slammed the door, and locked it. She sat for a minute, her breath heaving as if she had run a ten-mile race.

Don't be stupid. You're letting this get to you. She started the car and turned the headlights on. There was nothing around but a dark and lonely campus. *But someone is there. I'm sure of it.* She drove out of the lot, looking hard at the bushes on the side of the road as she left.

When she got to the stop sign at the end of Baker Street, she stopped the car and tapped an icon on her phone.

"Hey. What happened to you?" Cece's voice was light and airy. "I thought you were going to drop by the rehearsal."

"Sorry. Something came up.".

"You sound out of breath. Is everything okay?"

"Everything's fine." Kate was beginning to convince herself she was the victim of an overactive imagination. "I found out something interesting today."

"Oh? Tell me."

"Are you at home?"

"Yes."

"Great. I'll be there in fifteen minutes. We can look into this together."

When she arrived, Cece was waiting at the front door. "You figured something out?"

"No, but I think we took a step in the right direction. And it came from an unlikely source."

"Who?"

"Reen and Joanie."

"You're kidding," Cece said. "They actually gave you some information?"

Kate told her sister about the two girls and their episode in the library.

Cece's eyes grew wide when Kate mentioned silver.

"I don't know if they were genuinely frightened or really thrilled that they had such an exciting adventure, but the thing Andrew said about silver sounds like it could be related to the clue Reverend Whitefield found. What do you think it could mean?"

"Tell me again. What did Andrew say to the girl?"

"He said, 'What's the matter? I'm not as important as silver?' At least that's what they thought he said." She shook her head. "What can that mean?"

"Doesn't make any sense to me. How important is silver?" Cece plopped down on the sofa. "I'm not sure that's much of a clue."

"It sounds more like a boyfriend saying he's jealous because the girl likes somebody who's more important." She stood and snapped her fingers. "Of course. It's not the metal. It's a person's name."

"Yes!" Cece clapped her hands. "I bet you're right. Do you think there's a professor named Silver at the university?"

"I bet there is." Kate grabbed her laptop and opened up the home page for the university. "Faculty search," she said and started to type. "Nope. No faculty member named Silver. Rats."

"How about somebody in the administration or on the staff?" Cece asked.

"Looks like the search includes all of them. Dead end." Kate closed the laptop and hunched over it.

"Now what do we do?" Cece asked.

"This is getting too complicated for us. I think it's time to go to the police."

Chapter Twenty-Six

THE DETECTIVES

Detectives Carlioni and MacMillan had just returned from lunch when Carlioni found a message on his desk. "Oh no."

"What?" MacMillan asked.

Carlioni looked up at his partner and waved the slip of paper at him. "I got a call from Kathryn Frasier. She wants to talk about the fire at the library." He sank down into his desk chair. "Can't we do something to get rid of that woman?"

MacMillan chuckled and propped himself on the edge of his partner's desk. "You have to admit, Carli, she's pretty smart. If it hadn't been for her, we'd have put the wrong person on trial for Tinnerman's murder, and that would have made the whole department look bad—especially us." He picked up the Rubik's Cube from the corner of the desk and twisted it a few times. "We should be thanking her for what she did."

"She got lucky," Carlioni muttered. "Now she's all full of herself and wanting to prove there's a murder every time something unusual happens around here."

"A fire in the library where somebody dies isn't just an unusual thing, Carli." MacMillan ran a hand through his thick, sandy-colored hair. "I thought it was suspicious all along."

"Yeah, well, you were here when I asked Samantha Simpkins to let us reopen the case and you heard her say 'NO!' over the phone like she was practicing for the Olympic shouting competition. Besides, we got our plate full with our own work." Carlioni shifted in his chair and shrugged. "Kathryn Frasier will just have to find somebody else to help her."

There was a knock at the door. Carlioni put his head in his hands. "Please don't let that be her."

MacMillan opened the door "Hey, look who's here, Carli. It's Kathryn and Cece," he said and turned to Carlioni.

"We were just in the neighborhood," Kate said. "We thought we'd drop by to let you know what we found out about the fire in the library at the university."

"Hey, that's nice of you," MacMillan said and swung his arm to gesture them in. "Don't you think that's nice, Carli?" He raised his eyebrows and gave a silly grin to his partner.

Carlioni's eyelids drooped. "Look, Kathryn, the library fire is not our case. Telling us what you found won't help." He shook his head. "Besides, me and Mac are knee-deep in the Malone case, and we don't have any time to help you on your ... um, quest."

"What's the Malone case?" Cece asked.

Carlioni sighed. *Why did I go and mention that? Now they're going to head down a whole new rabbit hole.* "Look, I can't get into specifics of our investigation, but I can tell you what's been publicly reported."

"Thanks," Kate said.

Carlioni leaned on his desk. "Dr. Malone was chairman of the computer science department at the university. He was riding his bicycle home one night a few months ago and was struck by an automobile. It was a hit-and-run, and we don't have any suspects."

"That's terrible," Kate said. "Was he killed?"

"No," MacMillan answered. "When the car hit him, it knocked the bike off the road and down the side of a hill. He was seriously injured, but he'll live."

"Do you think it could have been intentional?"

Carlioni frowned. "We don't know. We've been doing background checks on all his colleagues. Dr. Malone was not well-liked among the faculty and students. He had a way of alienating just about everybody he knew, so it could have been anybody."

"We've checked everybody we could find who had a relationship with him," MacMillan said. "It should be easy to identify the car, but we came up empty." He shrugged. "It's looking more and more like a hit-and-run by someone who wasn't from around here."

"So is that why Dr. Penterson is the interim chairman of the department?" Kate asked.

"You got it." Carlioni took a mechanical pencil out of his pocket and twirled it around. "It's been quite a turnover there in the last few years. Malone took over when that other guy left." He squinted at his partner. "What was his name, Mac?"

"Silva," MacMillan said. "Dr. Silva was the chairman of the computer science department before Malone took over."

Chapter Twenty-Seven

IT'S SILVA!

"Silver?" Kate felt her heart jump. "Did you say 'Silver'?" she asked MacMillan.

"I said Silva. S-I-L-V-A." MacMillan looked at her like she had two heads. "Why?"

"That's it!" Cece said. She and Kate did a fist bump.

"It wasn't Silver. It was Silva." Kate laughed and clapped her hands.

MacMillan and Carlioni exchanged a look. "Care to tell us what's so exciting about Silva?" Carlioni asked.

"Remember we told you we were looking into a prayer request that might have had to do with Mr. Tyme's death?"

"How could we forget?" Carlioni snorted.

"Reverend Whitefield found another prayer request that had to do with silver. It must be referring to Dr. Silva."

"Whoa," MacMillan said. "That's a pretty big jump. How did you get there?"

Kate held her hands out, palms up. "Don't you see? Somebody is going after the chairmen of the computer science department."

"And that has to do with Mr. Tyme because ...?" Carlioni raised his eyebrows in mock anticipation.

"I don't know, but they must be related," Kate said.

"Look, Miss Frasier." Carlioni put the pencil in his shirt pocket. "I know you want to help, but you have a way of making connections that just aren't there." He stood. "Now I agree there was a crime committed when Dr. Malone was injured. It was definitely a hit-and-run. That's an open case, and Mac and I are working it." He walked around to the front of his desk. "But this other stuff about Mr. Tyme and Dr. Silva is just circumstantial. There's nothing there."

"No. You're wrong, detective," Kate said.

Carlioni's face turned such a dark shade of crimson, Kate was afraid he might explode. He pointed a finger at her. "Now listen here, young lady—"

MacMillan put his hand on his partner's outstretched arm. "Let's hear what she has to say, Carli." He turned to Kate. "Go ahead with your theory, Kathryn."

Kate walked over to a whiteboard on the wall. She wrote three words at the left side of the board, top to bottom: Silva, Malone, Tyme. Next to Silva she wrote: "Remove the dross from the silver." Beside Tyme she wrote: "Pour coals on his head." Next to Malone she put a big question mark.

She stepped back and pointed to the board. "Three university bigwigs were injured or killed, and we know there were prayer requests that seem to point to two of them."

"There's one little problem with your theory." Carlioni stepped up and picked up a red marker from the tray at the bottom of the whiteboard. He drew a big, red "X" over Silva's name. "Dr. Silva wasn't injured or killed. As a matter of fact, the reason Dr. Malone took his place was because Silva got promoted to some big position." He turned to MacMillan. "What was it, Mac?"

MacMillan looked back at his notes. "Here it is. Dr. Silva got named chancellor of the university, and Dr. Malone was given the position of Chairman of Computer Science." He dropped the folder back on his desk. "Sorry, Kathryn."

Kate gazed at the whiteboard. "There's something there. I just know it."

"Look, folks." Carlioni dropped the red marker back in the tray. "We can't chase every prayer request somebody drops in a box. That's not our territory." He brushed his hands together. "Besides, our temporary boss has already given us our marching orders. She wants us to concentrate on the Malone case. We take our orders from her."

"Her?" Kathryn asked.

"Our interim commissioner is Samantha Simpkins," MacMillan said.

"Maybe you should talk to her if you want to reopen the fire investigation." Carlioni seemed unusually cooperative.

"That's great. Thanks," Cece said.

"No problem." Carlioni held the door for them. "Her office is at the end of the hall." He pointed to the right. "You can't miss it." He closed the door quietly behind them

"That wasn't nice, Carli," MacMillan said. "You just sent those two into the lion's den."

"Yeah, I know." Carlioni took the mechanical pencil out of his pocket, tossed it on his desk, and laughed out loud.

Chapter Twenty-Eight

SAMANTHA SIMPKINS

"Hi. We'd like to see Samantha Simpkins, please." Kate addressed the tired-looking police officer sitting at the desk outside the office at the end of the hall. The nameplate said Officer Emerson.

"What do you want to see her about?" he asked.

"We have some information that might bear on a case the police department is working on." Kate smiled warmly.

"You can go online and fill out the citizen's information form. It will be routed to the appropriate department." He dropped his eyes back down to the newspaper he was reading.

Kate and Cece exchanged a look, and Kate stood up straighter. "This is about a possible murder. I think the commissioner will want to hear this."

The policeman yawned and took out a yellow pad. "Okay. Give me the details and I'll pass it on to Ms. Simpkins."

"It would really be helpful if we could talk to her directly," Kate said. "Commissioner Blake always met with us when we had concerns about something in the community."

"You met with Commissioner Blake?" He looked skeptical.

"Yes."

"That's nice," he said. "Ms. Simpkins has her own methods. Just give me the facts."

Cece stepped up to his desk. "Look," she said, "this is important."

"Yeah, yeah." His voice was a flat line. "It's all important, sister."

Cece opened her mouth, but before she could respond, the office door popped open, and an attractive young woman rushed out.

She wore navy blue slacks and a white blouse with sleeves pushed up to her elbows. Her shoulder-length, dark blonde hair was tucked back behind ears that displayed small loop earrings. She didn't acknowledge Kate or Cece in any way, but focused stern eyes on the policeman behind the desk.

Kate got a whiff of expensive perfume as the woman clacked by her in red stiletto heels and dropped a pile of papers on the policeman's desk. "Take care of these, Lonnie," she said without expression, and turned to go back into the office.

Kate grasped the opportunity. "Ms. Simpkins?"

The woman stopped and swung around. With her hand on the doorknob to her office, she looked at her watch and said, "Yes. What is it?"

Kate stepped up and held out her hand. "I'm Kathryn Frasier, and this is my sister, Cece Goldman." She nodded toward Cece. "Can we have a minute of your time?"

The woman ignored her hand and said in a dull voice, "You'll have to arrange an appointment with Lonnie. I'm very busy today." She turned again.

"It's about a murder."

Simpkins stopped again and slowly turned around. She frowned and looked directly at Kate for the first time. "What murder?"

"If we could just get a few minutes of your time, we can explain it." Kate saw the woman's jaw tighten as she looked back and forth between her and Cece.

Then she jerked her head toward the office. "All right. Come in, but you'll have to make it fast. I'm meeting with the mayor this afternoon and I have to prepare."

As they moved toward the office, Kate felt Cece's elbow poke into her side. Two nudges. Success.

Simpkins didn't offer them a chair. As she walked behind her desk, the phone buzzed.

Still standing, she picked up the landline and punched a button. "Yes." Her voice was clipped and irritable. "All right. Tell him I'll have something this afternoon." She hung up. "I need to finalize my report, so please make this quick." She deposited herself into the black leather executive chair.

"Ms. Simpkins, as the interim police commissioner, you need to be aware of what we've found," Kate began. "We know Detectives Carlioni and MacMillan are looking into the hit-and-run accident of Dr. Malone from the university."

"And?"

"We believe the fire at the university library may be related."

Simpkins picked up a paper on her desk and appeared to be reading it. Without looking up, she said, "The university fire was an accident. That investigation is closed."

"Yes, but—"

"No buts. If you have direct evidence of a crime being committed, you can give a written report to Lonnie." She pointed toward the door where the policeman sat. "Officer Emerson."

"We don't exactly have hard evidence," Cece said. "But there are suspicious circumstances we think should be investigated."

Simpkins made a large check mark on the paper she was holding and dumped it into the out-box. Then she picked up another one. "There's an online form to fill out for any concerns you may have." She duplicated the check mark on the second sheet and tossed it into the out-box.

The phone rang again, and Simpkins lifted the receiver. "Yes?" She paused and knitted her eyebrows together in a frown. She turned her chair to face the wall and held the phone in her left hand while her right hand fiddled with her earring.

"Thank you, Mr. Mayor. I'm working on that case now and we'll have a resolution this week. I promise. You can count on me." There was another long pause, then she said, "Yes, sir. I'm definitely on board." She swung the chair around, jammed the receiver back into its holder, and looked up as if surprised Kathryn and Cece were still there.

"You'll have to excuse me. I have work to do." Simpkins began to type on the laptop on her desk.

"If you'll just give us a minute to explain," Kate said.

Simpkins looked up. "I am a very busy woman." She put an equal emphasis on each word. "I don't have time to deal with every person who comes in here with a theory about crime. I have a tight schedule and an important list of things to do." She held up a piece of paper as if it were evidence of an overactive inbox, then she waved dismissively. "And I need to make progress. Good day."

Chapter Twenty-Nine

KATE ATTENDS CHAPEL

"We're getting nowhere," Kathryn said as she and Phil held hands and walked toward the chapel in the Saturday twilight. "That interim police commissioner pretty much told us to get lost." She stopped and looked up at him. "Reverend Whitefield was depending on me, and I feel like a failure."

Phil squeezed her hand. "Don't be so hard on yourself. You've done everything you could. Reverend Whitefield can't expect you to do miracles."

"Maybe a miracle is what I need." She heard the music while they were still twenty yards away and she turned to Phil. "We're a little late. They've already started singing."

When they got close to the door of the chapel, she saw movement at the right side of the building. A man slipped out of the shadows. She recognized the floppy hat and khaki shirt and pants. He looked furtively around and entered through the side door of the chapel.

She stopped cold and gasped.

Phil turned to her. "What?"

"A man just went into the door at the back of the church. I think it was Zachary Venero."

"The gardener you told me about?"

"Yes. The only thing back there is a hall and the robe room where the minister and the choir can put on their robes before the service. And there's a storage room where they keep a lot of the supplies for the chapel. Why would he be going in there during the service?" She felt her hands get cold. "I don't like this."

Phil stopped and looked down at her. "Let's don't assume there's something sinister happening. He could just be putting something in the storage room. We'll ask Reverend Whitefield about it after the service."

"Maybe we should go back there and check on what he's doing." Kate moved toward the side of the building.

"No." Phil held her hand. "We're not going to follow someone into the back of the chapel just because you've been thinking about your investigation. Come on. We're going to the service."

Kate lagged behind Phil, and she felt her heart rate bump up to another level.

They entered through the front foyer and stood in one of the pews in the back of the small chapel. The congregation was on the last stanza of "Great Is Thy Faithfulness," and Kate mouthed the words, but she couldn't concentrate on the music. What was Venero doing?

Reverend Whitefield took to the pulpit and smiled at the assembly. His face still held the melancholy expression she had noticed several days before, but he stood erect with his hands on each side of the lectern. "Today's lesson is from the gospel of Matthew, Chapter Seven." He opened the large Bible that sat on the pulpit and read from it.

"Judge not, that you be not judged. For with the judgment you pronounce, you will be judged, and with the measure you use, it will be measured to you. Why do you see the speck that is in your brother's eye, but do not notice the log that is in your own eye? Or how can you say to your brother, 'Let me take the speck out of your eye,' when there is the log in your own eye? You hypocrite, first take the log out of your own eye, and then you will see clearly to take the speck out of your brother's eye."

The minister looked up from the text and surveyed the congregation. "Do you suppose Jesus is teaching us to ignore sin?" He paused and let his gaze travel through the assemblage. "I don't think so. I believe he was talking to the religious leaders who were quick to condemn others for small things, but they ignored their own pride. They puffed themselves up on their knowledge of Scripture but missed the bigger picture of love and service."

Kate watched the door that connected the sanctuary to the rooms behind the altar. Was Venero back there? He was so strange. Could he be dangerous? Would he come charging out through that door brandishing a gun? She turned her attention to the windows on the side of the chapel. She should be able see anybody who left through the side door.

Bang! Kathryn jumped. Someone had dropped a hymnal on the floor. Phil looked down at her and mouthed, "Are you okay?"

She nodded and took a deep breath.

Reverend Whitefield continued, and Kathryn felt he was looking right at her. "The text continues," he said, "with these words: 'Ask, and it will be given to you; seek, and you will find; knock, and it will be opened to you. For everyone who asks receives, and the one who seeks finds, and to the one who knocks it will be opened.'" He smiled. "We should never give up our search for the truth."

Kathryn leaned toward Phil and whispered, "I wish I could find out the truth about why Mr. Venero was sneaking into the back door of the chapel."

Phil squeezed her hand and whispered back, "Maybe you will."

When the sermon ended and the congregation began singing the closing hymn, Kathryn saw the side door open. Venero stepped outside and walked away. She nudged Phil and nodded toward the window.

After the service, Kate put her hand on Phil's arm. "I'm going to check the room behind the altar," she said as she brushed past him into the side aisle.

"Wait. I'll come with you." He followed as she rushed down the aisle. Jan Whitefield was standing just in front of the first row, and she made eye contact with Kate and lifted her eyebrows. There was no question about what she was thinking. Why would Kathryn make a beeline to the robe room?

There was no choir in the Saturday evening service, so the robe room was empty. Kate stood in the middle of it and did a full 360-degree turn. Everything seemed to be in place. She moved the hangers one by one and felt the choir robes.

"What are you doing?" Phil stood with his arms crossed over his chest.

"I need to check everything in this room. Maybe Venero planted something here. He might be after Reverend Whitefield as his next victim."

She opened the cabinet where the hymnals were stored. “He was acting so odd.”

Phil pulled her to him and held her by the shoulders. “You’re the one acting odd. You need to get a grip on yourself.”

“But don’t you see ...” Before she could finish, the door opened and Reverend Whitefield stepped in.

“Ah,” he said. “Two of my favorite congregants. I don’t usually have company back here when I take off all the accoutrements of the ministry.” He unzipped the black robe, slipped it off, and carefully hung it on an empty hanger. “Jan told me she saw you rushing back here. Is anything wrong?” He gave a gentle smile. “I don’t suppose you’re looking to join the choir.”

“Kathryn was worried about something,” Phil said.

“Oh?”

Kate took a deep breath. “I saw Mr. Venero slip into the robe room and stay there all during the service. I thought maybe he left something here. You know, something’s not right about him.”

The minister’s face turned somber. “Let’s go back to the rectory and we’ll tell you about Zack.”

Chapter Thirty

WHO IS ZACHARY VENERO?

Kathryn helped Jan pour tea and took the platter into the living room of the rectory. Phil and Jim Whitefield stood at one of the bookcases, where Jim was pointing out some of his reference books.

After they had settled into their places, the reverend said, "I understand you were concerned about Mr. Venero, Kathryn."

"Yes. We saw him going into the side door behind the altar when we arrived. I think he stayed back there all during the sermon. Why would he do that?"

The reverend and his wife exchanged glances. "You needn't be worried," Jan said. "Zack is not a dangerous person."

Kate was surprised. "If somebody sneaks into the robe room during service, shouldn't we be concerned?"

"No." Reverend Whitefield's voice was firm. "Jan, why don't you tell them about Zack."

Jan's expression was somber. "Zack Venero was a brilliant young student back in the early seventies. He was sought after by several prestigious universities because of his talent in math and science. However, he decided he would prefer to go into the ministry." She paused to take a sip of tea. "But the Vietnam War was raging at that time, and Zachary felt it was his duty to serve his country before he followed his chosen profession." She stopped and looked at her hands.

"He was injured?" Phil asked.

"Yes." Jan looked up at them and her eyes were moist. "In more ways than one. He and his best friend were on patrol when they were ambushed by the Vietcong. They were both wounded, but his friend died before a medic could get to them. Zack spent months in an army hospital recovering from his own head wound, but the combination of things took a terrible toll on him."

She sighed and took a deep breath. "He had always been a serious thinker and a quiet person, but when he returned to the States, he seemed to collapse in on himself. No one knows if it was the physical injury or the psychological shock of his friend's death that affected him. Maybe it was a combination of both, but he was never able to function at the same level again. His parents took him in and cared for him for many years."

"Oh, how sad," Kate said. "Did they live here in Bellevue?"

"Yes. His father was Jonathan Venero, a member of the Board of Trustees of the university here." Jan nibbled on a cookie. "After Zack's mother died, Jonathan drew up a will that left his entire estate to the university on the stipulation that the trustees would provide a place for Zack to live and work for the rest of his life. The board agreed, and President Yarborough has been very helpful. They even renovated the small cottage behind the library for Zachary to live in after his father died."

"So Mr. Venero has been working as a gardener since then?" Kate asked.

"Yes." Jan smiled weakly. "His parents noticed his interest in caring for the plants around their home after he returned, and they encouraged his efforts. You can see what a wonderful gardener he is. And he still has his mechanical expertise as well. They say he can fix anything that's broken, and he's become something of a handyman as well as gardener. In spite of his quiet nature, the administration has a great deal of trust in him."

"I'll attest to his talents," the reverend said. "When our washing machine stopped working, Zack overheard me telling someone I was going to call a repairman, and he asked if he could look at it. He did and fixed it." He shook his head.

Jan spoke up. "He has a little toolshed behind his cottage where he keeps all manner of tools and things. He's one of those people who can do anything." Her voice became soft. "Except communicate. He seems to have developed a fear of relationships. It's a classic case of someone who lost a dear friend and is afraid of putting himself in that situation again because he might suffer another injury. You've noticed how he doesn't like to converse with people."

"Yes. I took it to mean he was angry, but I guess I misjudged him." Kathryn felt her face grow warm. "Maybe I should listen to your sermon again." She looked intently into the reverend's eyes. "Does that explain why he didn't come into the church to hear your sermon?"

Reverend Whitefield nodded. "Zack often goes into the robe room and listens to the sermon from there. He feels more comfortable being alone than sitting with the congregation."

Kate still wasn't satisfied. "But don't you think someone who has been severely damaged could pose a danger to others?"

The reverend shook his head. "A lot of people misjudge Zack because of the way he looks and his tendency to avoid contact with other people. But they just don't understand him. Beneath the exterior, there is a sensitive and brilliant man. A caring man. I don't believe Zack could be a danger to anyone."

Chapter Thirty-One

WHAT WOULD NANCY DREW DO?

"Maybe we should give up trying to find the murderer and do something else." Joanie was sitting on the bed in my room while we "rested" after lunch. "I'm getting scared."

I walked back and forth between the bed and the door and made my face look grown-up. "My dad said there's nothing to be afraid of. He says Andrew is just a meanie, but he's not going to hurt us."

"But we haven't figured anything out." Joanie hopped off the bed and straightened the spread where she had wrinkled it. "And your dad said we have to stop investigating Mr. Tyme's death and find something else to do."

"We have a duty to perform." I planted my hands on my hips and tried to look like Wonder Woman. "Poor Mr. Tyme deserves nothing less than for us to find his murderer, and we're going to do it." Emphatic nod.

Joanie opened my closet door and started straightening the pile of shoes inside. "Our plan isn't working. Nobody wants to talk to us about campus buildings."

"Hmm. That's a good point." I walked over to the bookcase and fingered the spines of some of the books. "What would Nancy Drew do?"

Joanie started to hum as she moved things around in the closet.

"Let's think about the people we talked to so far," I said. "Mrs. Toussaint isn't any help. She'll just get mad if we ask her about Mr. Tyme."

"How about Miss Culberson?" Joanie picked up one of my sandals and was searching through the rest of the shoes to find a match.

"We can't talk to her. She's our prime suspect."

Joanie found the other sandal and pulled it out. She clapped the shoes together. "What's a prime suspect?"

"It's the person we think probably did the deed," I said and raised one of my eyebrows sharply. I learned how to do that last year.

"Oh." She carefully laid the sandals on one side of the closet.

"And we can't talk to Andrew because he's mad at us and he probably wouldn't tell us the truth, anyway."

"Um." I could tell Joanie wasn't listening to me anymore.

"We can't talk to Dad or Kathryn because they want us to stop our investigation." I flopped back on the bed and stared at the ceiling. "We need to find somebody who knows a lot about the university and won't be mean to us." The fan on the ceiling turned round and round while the air currents drifted down around me. "That's it!" I leaped up. "Dr. Drafton!"

I shouted so loud that Joanie jumped and stopped rearranging the shoes. She looked at me. "Who?"

"Dr. Drafton. He's this old guy. He's sort of a distant relative of my mom's, and my dad visits him sometimes. He took me with him a couple of times. Dad says Dr. Drafton knows everything about the university."

"What does Dr. Drafton do?"

I shrugged. "I don't know. He used to be something at the university, but now he's retired."

Joanie made that "mmm" sound she always uses when she doesn't like what I'm telling her. "We're not supposed to get involved, Reen. Your dad said so."

I grabbed my notebook and pen. "C'mon. We're going to solve the murder and become famous." I pulled her arm until she stood up. "He lives in a spooky old house across the street from the library. I bet he even saw something."

Chapter Thirty-Two

DR. DRAFTON

"I don't like this house. It smells funny." Joanie wrinkled up her nose like she got a whiff of rotten eggs.

"Old houses always smell that way." I rang the doorbell.

Joanie ran her finger down the cracked paint next to the front door. Everything seemed gray and dull. "I don't think he's home," she said. "Let's go." She started backing away from the door.

I grabbed her hand. "No. He's just old. It probably takes him a long time to get to the door." I rang the doorbell again. "Now remember, we won't mention Mr. Tyme right away. We'll just talk about university buildings. We have to be subtle."

"What's subtle?" Joanie asked.

"It means we can't say anything about the murder." I was just about to explain more when the door opened a little crack, and I could see an eye peering out at me. It was an old, wrinkly eye.

"Are you selling Girl Scout cookies?" he said.

"No sir."

"Oh. That's too bad. I love Girl Scout cookies." He opened the door a little farther and I could see both eyes and the rest of him too. Dr. Drafton was short and stooped over. He didn't have much hair, but what he had was gray and messed up, like he just got out of bed. "Are you selling something else?" he said.

"No sir. We want to interview you." I tried to look interesting. "Maybe you remember me. I'm Nate Penterson's daughter."

He reached in his shirt pocket and pulled out a pair of glasses. "So you are! You're Irene. I remember when you came to see me last year." His face was still wrinkled, but his eyes got brighter. Maybe nobody had ever interviewed him before. He looked at Joanie. "And who is she?"

"This is my cousin, Joanie. She's helping me." I tried to sound super polite, the way Mrs. Toussaint says I should speak to grown-ups. "We're writing a paper for school about the buildings on campus, and my father said you know everything about the university. Could we interview you?"

He hesitated, and I thought he was going to tell us to go away, but he was just trying to unlatch the screen door. "Well, I'm impressed," he said. "Most children these days can't seem to do much but play with their phones." He pushed the door. It scraped the bottom of the threshold, but he finally got it open far enough so we could go inside. "Come in. I'd be delighted to talk to you."

Joanie and I looked at each other. She mouthed, "Wow." Somebody wanted to talk to us!

The rooms in Dr. Drafton's house were huge, and it was dark inside. Joanie reached over and grabbed my arm.

Dr. Drafton was wearing bedroom slippers, and he shuffled ahead of us. "Come into the living room. I'll turn on some lights."

When Dr. Drafton flipped the light switch, I gasped and Joanie started to scream, but she clapped her hand over her mouth so fast it came out like a squeak. Standing in the living room next to the fireplace was a knight in shining armor. Really.

Dr. Drafton chuckled. "Ever seen a suit of armor before?" he said when he saw our faces.

"No." I moved around the side of the knight and reached out to touch the spear he was holding. "Is it real?"

"Yes!" Dr. Drafton looked like he came alive. "It's a real suit of armor from the twelfth century. Belonged to a knight in England. I just had it delivered from a museum in Cleveland."

"He was big," Joanie said and peeked around the back. "How did he put it on?"

"With a lot of difficulty," Dr. Drafton said and laughed.

"Why did you want a knight, Dr. Drafton?" I was beginning to wonder if Dr. Drafton had gone a little daffy after he retired.

"That's a good question, Reen. It's a symbol."

Joanie touched the stomach of the knight and gave it a little push. "Why did people wear armor?"

"Ah, now there's a question we could discuss for years!" Dr. Drafton seemed really excited. I thought he was beginning to get younger, and I wondered if he was some kind of wizard. "In some ways, we all wear a suit of armor."

"I don't," Joanie said and poked out her lip.

"I don't mean real armor, but we all try to look good to other people, so we wear something to make them think good things about us."

"You mean like a costume?" Joanie likes costumes.

"Yes!" Dr. Drafton looked at Joanie like she had just won the *Jeopardy! Tournament of Champions*. "You're a very smart little girl." Joanie's face turned real pink and she looked like she was glowing.

Dr. Drafton shuffled down the hall. "Let's go in the kitchen and we can discuss knights and armor. Would you girls like a glass of lemonade?"

"Yes. Thank you." Joanie is also a big fan of lemonade.

We followed him into the kitchen. It was an old-timey kitchen, like the ones you see in movies. Everything was big. There was a huge gas stove at one end of the room and a monster refrigerator against the wall. The kitchen table was right in the middle of the room, and we sat around it while Dr. Drafton got the lemonade out of the refrigerator and told us about the knight.

"Did he kill people?" I asked.

"I suppose he did. There was a lot of killing going on back then, you know."

"But the armor kept him from being killed?" I drank some of the lemonade. It was really good. He must have made it fresh.

"Yes," he said. "Armor protected the knight."

"But wasn't it awfully hot and heavy for him to walk around in?" Joanie asked. She wrinkled up her nose. "I wouldn't want to wear something like that."

"You girls are so smart!" Dr. Drafton looked like he really meant it. "You've just realized that wearing armor can protect you from harm, but it can be very difficult to carry around." He crossed his arms over his chest and looked really satisfied with himself. "That was true a thousand years ago, and it's still true today."

Then I remembered. Dad said Dr. Drafton was a psychology professor.

"As a matter of fact, you're so smart, I think you should have a cookie to go along with your lemonade." He hopped up from his chair like he had just acquired a jolt of energy, pulled down a cookie jar from the shelf over the counter, and put it on the table. He took the top off the jar. "Go ahead and take what you want."

I leaned over and looked in. I thought there would be a lot of stale Fig Newtons, and I was ready to say I wasn't hungry. But instead, the jar was full of all sorts of luscious-looking cookies. "Wow, Dr. Drafton. These look good. Did you make them?" I took a bite and the cookie just kind of melted around my teeth.

"I have a lady friend who brings me cookies now and then." He smiled a really cute little grin and I think he blushed. "You may know her. She's a librarian on campus. Miss Culberson."

"Miss Culberson?" Joanie blurted it out like it was the title of a hit song. "We think she—"

I kicked her hard under the table, and she looked at me, all surprised. "We think she's nice," I said, trying to look innocent. "Here, Joanie, try one of these." I handed her a big chocolate chip cookie. I figured that would keep her busy for a while.

Dr. Drafton looked suspicious, and he shifted his eyes back and forth between us. My dad said psychology professors are always trying to read your mind because that's what they do for a living. I don't think Dr. Drafton got much out of Joanie's mind because she took the cookie and sat back in the chair, taking little nibbles like a bird.

He turned his face to me. I pretended to be really interested in the cookie jar so I wouldn't have to look at him. Maybe they can't read your mind if you're not looking at them.

"So let's talk some more about why people have armor." Dr. Drafton rubbed his hands together like he was getting warmed up, and I had a bad feeling he was about to give us a lecture. "Joanie, why do you suppose people wear armor?"

"To keep from getting hurt." As she swung her legs, she bounced up and down on her chair, looking really satisfied with herself. "It's too bad Mr. Tyme wasn't wearing armor."

I kicked Joanie again and she squealed, "Stop kicking me."

"Mr. Tyme?" Dr. Drafton looked super interested.

"We think he got murdered," she said.

It's clear to me that Joanie doesn't need a psychologist to read her mind. She just dumps it out there for the whole world to see.

Chapter Thirty-Three

LET'S SOLVE THIS MYSTERY

"You think Mr. Tyme was murdered?" Dr. Drafton asked Joanie, but he was looking at me.

Uh-oh. Now we're in for it. Time to throw out a smoke screen.

"We were just playing a game," I said. I decided not to kick Joanie again. It would just make things worse. "Joanie didn't mean it was a real murder." I frowned at her so she'd get the message. "We're just pretending."

"Ah." He turned to Joanie. "Tell me about your game."

Joanie got that look like she gets when she wants to impress somebody. "Mr. Tyme died and the police think it was an accident, but we believe he was murdered and we're going to prove it."

Dr. Drafton suddenly looked a lot younger. Like he had just time traveled while we were sitting at the table. It made me wonder if time travel was real. "Maybe I could play your game with you. You know, I thought there was something suspicious about Mr. Tyme's death."

"You did?" Joanie and I both said it at the same time. This was the first adult who didn't try to talk us out of our theory.

"I saw the fire that night. Let's see." He scratched his almost bare head. "It must have been three or four weeks ago."

"It was about a month ago," I offered.

"You can see the back door of the library from my window. Come look," he said. He led us into the den that looked out of the back of his house and pointed out the window.

"Wow. That's amazing," I said. I felt like jumping up and down, but I tried to keep it under control so he wouldn't think I was acting like a kid. "Mr. Tyme's office is right inside that door."

"I know. The police came over and asked if I had seen anything suspicious that night."

"Did you?" Joanie had forgotten all about her cookie.

"No. I was in bed." He blushed again, and I wondered why being in bed would make somebody blush. "But I heard the fire trucks when they came. It was quite exciting." He peered out the window. "Poor Mr. Tyme. Such a nice man. Did you see his office?"

"We tried to investigate, but they won't let us go in."

"Well, we'll just see about that," he said. "I'll be right back." He disappeared down the hall, and Joanie and I just looked at each other. I didn't know what to do. Dr. Drafton seemed a little strange to me, but Joanie was grinning like she'd just found the golden egg at an Easter egg hunt. She's a little naive.

Dr. Drafton reappeared, wearing regular clothes and shoes that looked like hiking boots. He was carrying a jacket and a hat. When he got to us, he put the hat on. It was one of those kinds that you see in old detective movies. He made a great show of slinging his jacket around before he put his arms in the sleeves. I could see the cleaning tag still pinned to the inside. When we got to the door, he took a walking stick out of the rack.

"Girls," he said, real dramatic-like. "Let's solve this mystery."

Chapter Thirty-Four

KINESTATIC

"We're kinestatic," Kate said glumly as she parked her car in the lot next to the drama department.

Cece looked over from the passenger seat. "We're *what?*"

"Kinestatic. You know, we're being kinetic by running around all over the place, but we're static because we're not getting anywhere. We're kinestatic."

"If you say so."

Kate bit on her bottom lip. "We need to get creative."

Cece looked dubious. "I'm not sure I like it when you get into a creative mode," she said. "Especially when we're talking about a murder."

"Look. Samantha Simpkins isn't going to help us, and she won't let Carlioni and MacMillan work on the case. She's washed her hands of it, so the police are out of it."

"Check." Cece nodded her head.

"If we're right ..."

"You mean if you're right," Cece said. "I'm not smart enough to have a theory."

"If *we're* right," Kate continued, ignoring Cece's objection, "then there were three victims—Silva, Malone, and Tyme."

"Sounds like a triple play."

Kate still ignored her sister. "We can't interview Tyme."

"Your powers of observation astound me."

"But we can interview Silva and Malone."

Cece frowned. "But that means we go from trying to decode a message to trying to solve a murder. Phil won't like that. Ben won't like it. Nobody will like it." She pointed a finger at herself. "Including me."

"Maybe not." Kate turned in her seat to look squarely at Cece. "But we decided before that the truth is important. I'm certain there's a connection between these two men and Mr. Tyme."

Cece sighed and took a deep breath. "I hate to say it, but you may be right."

"Look," Kate said, "this might sound corny, but we may be the only ones who can get to the bottom of this. If we don't do something, it's likely no one will ever know what happened to Mr. Tyme or to the others. We have to at least give it our best shot."

"Okay." Cece unfastened her seatbelt. "You've convinced me with your usual left-brain analysis." She plastered a *this-is-important* expression on her face and tilted her head to the right. "But I'm right-brained, and my intuition tells me we need to be cautious."

"Absolutely. We'll only talk to people on a need-to-know basis. While you're at rehearsal, I'll see about making an appointment with Dr. Silva. I'll just say we have some questions about the university he may be able to help with. If that prayer request really refers to him, there's got to be a reason." Kate opened her door and swung out of the car.

Cece hopped out of the passenger side. "So long, sister. I'm going to do something much harder than solving a murder."

"What's that?"

"I'm off to become a queen." She made a grand nose-in-the-air gesture and strutted off toward the theater. A few steps later, she turned with an impish grin on her face and waved.

Kate gave her a wave back and started toward the rectory when her phone rang. The caller ID showed Isabelle Cassidy.

"Dr. Cassidy, hi."

"Hello, Kathryn. Is this a good time to talk?"

"Yes." She leaned against the side of her car. "This is fine."

"I spent some time working with the code you gave me. I'm convinced it's a substitution cipher, but a sophisticated one."

"What do you mean?"

"I suspect the cryptographer used a special key so we wouldn't be able to decrypt it by the standard methods. If you can drop by my house, I'll show you what I mean."

"I'm just on my way to the rectory. I can stop by after that. Maybe an hour from now?"

"That would be fine."

Kate trudged slowly toward the rectory. If Dr. Cassidy couldn't figure out the code, what hope did she have?

As she neared the Whitefield's home, she saw Mr. Venero in the garden, his wheelbarrow full of fresh topsoil. A shovel leaned against the side of the house, and he tamped in the soil around the base of a large begonia plant. "Hi, Mr. Venero."

He looked over his shoulder and shaded his eyes. He tipped his hat, then turned back to his work.

Kate stood admiring his handiwork but unsure of whether to talk to him. Jan Whitefield's words came back to her. *Zack lives in his own world. It would be wrong to force him into ours.*

Venero stood and pushed the wheelbarrow along the path next to the garden. Kate noticed he dragged his right foot, making a scraping sound along the walkway.

The tower clock bell rang out two somber tones. Zack Venero wiped his forehead with the back of his hand, took the pocket watch out of his jacket, and stared at it as if it held some special meaning. Kate backed away quietly and rang the doorbell.

Jan Whitefield opened the door with her usual broad smile. "Glad you're here. Jim's been in his office all morning working on a sermon, and I think he's ready for a break. Come on in and let's have a snack."

Reverend Whitefield appeared at the door of his office and walked down the long hall toward her. "Ah, my favorite detective. How are we doing today?"

Jan shook her finger at him. "Now don't start interrogating her until I have a chance to get some tea and cookies out."

Kate held up her hand. "Nothing for me, thanks. Cece and I ate lunch a little while ago and I'm stuffed."

"Then come on in and let's talk." The reverend motioned toward the living room and Kate took a seat in one of the armchairs.

She gestured with her hands out, palms up. "I'm afraid I don't have much to report. Dr. Cassidy called to say she hadn't found anything. I'm going over to her house after this to talk to her."

"Too bad," the minister said. "I was hoping Dr. Cassidy would think of something."

Kate shook her head. "Cece and I tried to talk Detectives Carlioni and MacMillan into helping us, but they're working on another case, and the interim commissioner won't let them get involved with one that's already been closed."

"Ah," Reverend Whitefield said. "I thought it might be a losing battle, but we never know until we try. Sorry it didn't work out."

"We learned something new, though, that we thought might be important, but they poked holes in my theory."

"What's this new information?" the minister asked.

"We learned there was a Dr. Silva who was chairman of the computer science department, and we thought that might be what the 'silver' clue was referring to, but it doesn't look like that's the case."

"Why not?" Jan asked.

"We thought maybe someone was trying to murder high-ranking officials at the school, but they said Dr. Silva wasn't the victim of a murder attempt. They said he was actually promoted to chancellor."

"That's right," Jan said. "But he left the university a while back."

"He resigned?" Kate asked.

"Yes. It was around the end of last year." Jan rubbed her chin. "I don't want to spread rumors, but since we're talking about a possible crime, I believe he was asked to resign."

Kate leaned forward. "Why?"

"Don't repeat this," Jan said, "but I believe he was going to be investigated for sexual harassment."

Chapter Thirty-Five

VERBAL SUITS OF ARMOR

Kate expected the medical student to answer the doorbell, but instead Dr. Cassidy herself opened the door. She was leaning on a pair of forearm crutches.

"I can tell by your expression that you expected to see me in my wheelchair," Dr. Cassidy said. "I'm guessing you thought I am permanently disabled."

Kate felt her face grow warm with embarrassment. "You seem to know my mind better than I do, Dr. Cassidy. I feel foolish that I jumped to that conclusion."

"Actually, it's evidence of a positive personality trait."

"How can that be?"

"It means you haven't been investigating me—at least not my health status. Most people on campus could tell you I had an operation a little over a year ago. I've been recuperating slowly, but I'm getting better." She gestured with her head. "Come on in."

Kate stepped up into the foyer and closed the door behind her. As she followed the professor into the living room, she was surprised to see that Cassidy was as tall as she was. At five feet nine inches, Kate rarely met women she could look straight in the eyes.

The living room was bright and sunny with two large windows on the front wall. There was a long desk facing the windows and a plain brick fireplace on the adjacent wall. Bookcases lined the walls, and a Steinway grand piano stood in the far corner with the keyboard facing out.

Kate drifted toward the piano. "That's a beautiful instrument, Dr. Cassidy." She noted the older woman's unpolished, clipped fingernails.

"Do you play?" Cassidy asked.

"A little and very poorly," Kate said.

Dr. Cassidy's lips turned up in a wry smile. "But you're a fan of Jane Austen."

Kate felt a small electric shock flow through her. "Once again, you astound me by knowing something about me without my telling you."

"Ah, but you did tell me," Cassidy said. "You quoted a line from the movie version of *Pride and Prejudice* where Elizabeth Bennet says she plays the piano-forte 'a little and very poorly.' It's a famous line."

Kate shook her head. "I'm surprised the psychology department hasn't hired you. You seem to be able to read people's minds."

Dr. Cassidy managed to stand erect while leaning on the metal arm supports. "That was just an educated guess. You're an open and honest person, Kathryn. I could imagine you would be a fan of Austen's, and your comment seemed to confirm that." Her smile faded. "Most people run their thoughts through a self-protective filter before they convert them to words."

"Sort of like a code?"

"Exactly. Many people are defensive. They're concerned about the perception others have of them, so they hide behind a verbal suit of armor." Her face softened. "You haven't developed that armor yet, and I hope you never do." The professor fell silent.

Kate gazed into Cassidy's eyes and had a strange, melancholy sense of recognition, as if she were looking at an older version of herself. "You give me too much credit," she said softly.

Dr. Cassidy blinked and motioned toward the large desk with two chairs drawn up to it. "Have a seat." She eased herself into one of the chairs and propped the crutches against the wall.

A copy of the coal code was printed on a large piece of paper lying in the center of the desk. Dr. Cassidy ran a long, tapered index finger along the letters. "I suspect the cryptographer used a special key so we wouldn't be able to decrypt it by the standard means."

"How does that work?"

"They would probably use a phrase or set of words to map to the alphabet. For example, they could map 'The quick brown fox jumped over the lazy dog' to the alphabet. Only a person who knows the key could decipher the message." She pulled a sheet of paper out from under the coal code with the alphabet and the key written on it. "See here. This is the decrypted message when I used that sentence as the key. It's just nonsense letters."

"Oh, I see. So we can't decode it without the key?"

"Right. I tried some other commonly used keys. 'We the people of the United States' is one. Also, the first few words of the Declaration of Independence." She showed Kate some papers using each of the keys she had tried. "I went through about ten, but none of them worked."

"So it's hopeless?"

"Not necessarily. Can you think of any key that might have been used?"

Kate sat back in her chair. "Maybe a phrase that has the word 'time' in it since it has to do with Mr. Tyme."

"Great suggestion." Cassidy pulled her laptop to her. "I've written a program that maps words to the alphabet and uses that to decrypt the message. Let's try this one." She typed in the line "Now is the time for all good men to come to the aid of their country." The program stripped out duplicate letters and mapped the rest of the phrase to the alphabet.

The decrypted message was still a bunch of unintelligible letters.

"Too bad," Kate said. "But if the word 'time' is in the key, would it be possible to try all the combinations of ways that would map to the alphabet? Maybe that would get us closer."

"I could try that," Cassidy said, "but it may not work because some of the letters of the word 'time' may have been previously used in the key, and duplicate letters are generally stripped out." Cassidy sat back in her chair and squinted at the laptop. "However, I'll write a program to check out your idea. I can also gather sayings about time and run them through my program. If any of them work, we'll have solved the code."

"That's wonderful. But suppose they don't work?"

"Well, there are more sophisticated means of solving it. I know some people at the NSA, but I couldn't ask them to get involved unless we had proof that a crime had been committed."

"I understand." Kate tried not to let her voice give away the disappointment.

"I'll keep trying, but I don't want you to get your hopes up on this," Dr. Cassidy said. "The key could be anything, or it could be nonsense letters. If it contains the word 'time,' we may get lucky. I'll let you know if I come up with anything."

Chapter Thirty-Six

SEARCHING THE OFFICE

Dr. Drafton is definitely the coolest guy I ever knew. He marched across the street ahead of us looking real serious, and he stabbed the ground with his walking stick at every step.

When we got to the back door of the library, he pulled a key chain out of his pocket. There were just a few keys on it. Not like Mr. Venero's.

Dr. Drafton fiddled with the keys. His hands are kind of gnarly, so he had trouble separating them. Then he got the right one. It looked just like the big gold key Mr. Venero had used. He held it up like it was a prize. "Master key," he said.

"You have a master key to the university?" I asked.

"Yes. All the department chairs have master keys. Once they give it to you, they never take it back." He cackled and poked the key into the slot. "University administration is so astute."

He opened the back door and we stepped into the hall. The door to Mr. Tyme's office was just on our left. The door was closed, and Dr. Drafton used the same key to open it.

"Ta-da!" he said. "Mr. Tyme's office is open for inspection. But let me go in first to make sure it's safe." He went in the room and walked around, checking it out. I guess they must have taken out all the papers and books because there wasn't much in the office. Just a bunch of shelves and a big desk in the middle of the room. When he finished his walk-around, he motioned for us to come in, then he closed the door and locked it.

"This is the first time I've ever been inside the room where a murder took place," I said, and I looked around, wondering what we should do now that we were in. "I bet there's a clue somewhere that tells us who killed Mr. Tyme."

Dr. Drafton put his walking stick by the doorframe. "We need a plan," he said. "We should look in the desk and on the shelves for clues. Which one do you girls want to search?"

"We'll take the desk," I said. There's always a clue in the desk.

"Okay, I'll take the shelves." Dr. Drafton was getting into this.

"What are we looking for?" Joanie asked.

"Anything that could be a clue," Dr. Drafton said. "If something looks out of place, let me know."

The desk was a big metal one. There wasn't a center drawer, so I told Joanie to take the drawers on the left and I took the ones on the right. There were just a few papers on my side and a book of crossword puzzles. I guess the fire didn't get inside the desk. Joanie's side was better. There were tools and office stuff.

Dr. Drafton ran his hands along each shelf. "I'm afraid there's not much here," he said. "The police must have removed everything from the shelves."

Joanie was playing with the stapler. "I found some things," she said.

Dr. Drafton walked over and looked in the drawer. "Hmm." He rubbed his chin. "That's interesting."

"What?" Joanie and I both looked in the drawer.

"These are the kinds of tools we keep around when we need to do maintenance work at home or in the office." He picked each thing up and laid it on the top of the desk. "There's a tape measure, a pair of scissors, a ruler, a screwdriver, a hammer, and nails. I guess Mr. Tyme must have done some work around the office." He took the stapler from Joanie and added it to the pile on the desk.

Dr. Drafton put the things back in the drawer and looked like he was thinking. He squinted his eyes 'til they were almost shut and opened his mouth to say something when we heard a noise. Somebody was outside the office, trying to get in. They pushed at the door and jiggled the doorknob. Then we heard the sound of a key going into the keyhole.

Chapter Thirty-Seven

LILLY AND JOLLY

Dr. Drafton put his fingers to his lips like he was telling us to be quiet. Then he pointed to the desk and motioned for us to hide behind it while he walked around to the door. Joanie and I got down on our hands and knees and squeezed ourselves under the desk. I'm glad Joanie is little. Whoever it was wouldn't see us because the desk faced the door and there was a panel on the front side that hid us.

A *click* sounded in the door. Maybe the murderer was coming back to make sure he didn't leave any clues. Or maybe it was that big policeman.

Joanie squeezed my arm so tight it hurt, and her eyes got so big they just about took up all the room on her face. I put my finger to my lips, but my heart was beating so hard I was afraid everybody could hear it.

The door made a scratchy noise as it moved over the dirt and stuff on the floor, and I held my breath. I could just barely see the bottom of the door as it was pushed open and a pair of bright pink shoes walked in.

Miss Culberson!

The shoes stopped all of a sudden and there was a gaspy scream. I guess that's when she saw Dr. Drafton standing there. I bet her eyeglasses even fell down onto the bungee cord.

"Why, Lilly!" Dr. Drafton said, all friendly, like he just met her while he was out for a stroll. "How nice to see you."

Joanie and I looked at each other. Her mouth was wide open and so was mine.

I could see Dr. Drafton's feet move over right in front of Miss Culberson's feet. "Lilly, are you all right?"

She sounded like she was choking. She coughed and made a few little *umm* sounds before she got her voice back. "Jolly! You frightened me. What are you doing here?"

Jolly? Dr. Drafton's first name is Jolly?

"I was going to stop by to say hello to you when I decided to take a look at the scene of the crime," he said cheerfully.

"Crime?" she said. Her voice was doing that dance above high C again. "Jolly, this wasn't a crime. It was an accident."

Dr. Drafton's feet shuffled, and he dropped his voice like he was sharing a secret. "You know, there are some people who think Mr. Tyme was murdered."

"Jolly, you mustn't go around spreading such a rumor."

"Oh, don't worry. I won't say a thing. I just wanted to see how much damage there was." He paused. "What are you doing here, Lilly?"

She *ummed* some more. The pink shoes moved closer to the desk. I think she was leaning on it. "Oh, I guess I may as well tell you. I'm worried the police may reopen the investigation, and there's something here that might look bad for me."

"Oh?" I could imagine Dr. Drafton's face. I bet he time-traveled again. "What would that be, dear?" he said.

The hiking boots moved over, and they were standing very close now. Toe to toe.

"Well, you see, Clarence and I had a big argument the night he died. It was about a request I had put in to enlarge the preschool children's literature section."

"Preschool children's literature? In a university library?" he said.

"Yes. Childhood education is very important, and I've always been an advocate to provide as much preschool literature as possible in the library." I heard her sigh. "But Clarence said there was no budget this year and just refused to talk about it. I got so mad that I screamed at him and told him he should retire because he had gotten too old to do his job."

"Oh. That is serious. Did anyone hear you?"

"Everyone had already left, and we had locked the library, so I don't think anyone could have heard."

"So why be concerned about it? People lose their tempers all the time." Dr. Drafton's voice sounded all sweet and I could sense he was moving into his psychology role. I wondered if he was looking into her eyes and reading her mind.

Miss Culberson sounded like she was sniffling. "Oh, Jolly. I did something so childish. I yanked the proposal out of his hands and wrote something awful on the front of it."

"What did you write?"

I saw the pink shoes go wobbly.

"I need to sit down," she said, and the shoes walked over to an office chair next to the door. Dr. Drafton's hiking boots followed.

"I wrote 'Monster Tyme' and drew a stupid picture of a demon-looking thing with horns. Then I shoved it back at him, grabbed my purse, and left. After he died, I was afraid the police would find that paper and suspect me of murdering him." She sniffled louder. "I was so relieved when they didn't find it, but every now and then I get nervous and come back down here to look for it. Clarence was such a mysterious man. He may have hidden it somewhere. And I don't have an alibi for the night of the murder."

"That was the night you called and broke our date, wasn't it?"

Date? Dr. Drafton and Miss Culberson had a date?

"I was so angry, I went home and cried for hours. Oh, Jolly, this looks bad for me, doesn't it?"

"Now, now," I heard Dr. Drafton say. I think he was patting her shoulder. "I know you couldn't have murdered Mr. Tyme. You're getting upset over nothing. Go on upstairs and wash your face and I'll inspect this office with a fine-tooth comb. Then I'll come up and we'll talk."

The pink shoes stood up and all four feet walked toward the door.

It was dusty under the desk, and I felt like I was going to sneeze. I pinched my nose real hard so it wouldn't happen, but I could feel it coming on. Joanie knew it too because her eyes got even bigger than they were before. I put my hand over my nose and mouth and kept squeezing, but I couldn't help it. It was coming out.

Joanie shook her head and looked like she was going to panic.

I sneezed, but there was hardly any sound. Just a tiny snuffle.

The pink shoes stopped. "What was that noise?"

"What noise?" Dr. Drafton played dumb.

"I heard something over by the desk."

"It's probably just mice." Dr. Drafton used the old mouse trick. Good one. "You know they like to scurry around burned-out rooms."

Miss Culberson didn't seem to be afraid, but Joanie looked like she was going to jump up and run out if there were mice. I shook my head at her and silently mouthed, "No mice." She got the message.

"I think I should just check the desk again," Miss Culberson said. "That's the most likely place that horrible message would be and I'm not sure I was thorough before." The pink shoes started moving toward the desk.

"No, dear." The hiking boots caught up and turned her around. "I must insist. You're suffering from PTSD caused by the trauma of losing a friend and the effects of a guilty conscience. Remember, I'm the professional here, and the prescribed treatment is to refocus your mind. I insist that you go back upstairs and continue your regular work. You'll be surprised how much it will help."

Wow. Dr. Drafton sounded smart.

Miss Culberson muttered something like she didn't think it was a good idea, but the four shoes moved toward the door.

"And you can come over tonight after work and we'll see what we can do about that guilt complex." Dr. Drafton made a funny chuckle.

"Oh, Jolly." Miss Culberson sounded all cutesy. "I'll bring dessert."

"That sounds like a delicious idea," Dr. Drafton said and then Miss Culberson made a little *eek* sound and giggled. I didn't know librarians could giggle.

Then she said "Oh, Jolly" again, but in a really soft voice, and I wondered what was going on.

The two pairs of shoes stayed together for a long time. I was beginning to wonder if Dr. Drafton had forgotten about us when the pink shoes turned around and left and I heard the door close. The hiking boots walked over to the desk.

"All right, young ladies, you're safe to come out," he said.

I crawled out first. "I think she's lying," I said as I stood up. "I bet she's just trying to get rid of fingerprints or something."

Dr. Drafton took a handkerchief out of his pocket and wiped his mouth. "I assure you, Reen, Lillian Culberson couldn't do anything like that. She and I are ..." Dr. Drafton coughed and turned his head away from me. "... very good friends. I know her." He wiped his mouth again and I could see lipstick on the handkerchief. Pink lipstick.

"Ouch." Joanie had started to inch her way out from under the desk. "I hit my head."

The sound was a kind of *bong* and I laughed. "It sounds like you rang a bell," I said.

"Don't laugh, Reen," she said. "It isn't nice." Then she looked up at the bottom of the desk. "Wow. Look at this."

Chapter Thirty-Eight

THE CLUE

I got down on my hands and knees and looked at the bottom of the desk just above Joanie's head. There was an automobile license plate stashed underneath a couple of slats. A real license plate like the one on my dad's car. A clue!

I grabbed Dr. Drafton's hand. "Look! There's something here."

He made a big deal about having to get down on his hands and knees to look. He held on to the edge of the desk with one hand and put the other hand on my shoulder. Then he eased himself down to his knees. Maybe I'll buy him a pair of kneepads for Christmas.

Dr. Drafton put his hands on the floor and bent his head way to the side, peering underneath the desk where Joanie was still sitting. "That's odd," he said.

"Do you think it's a clue?" I couldn't wait to find out what it meant.

"I don't know." He reached in, but his arm wasn't long enough. "See if you can get it out."

I pulled on one end while Joanie pushed the other side, and we got it out from under the slats. Then we crawled out and helped Dr. Drafton get to his feet. He had to lean on both of us to stand up. He huffed a little, but he finally stood up straight and held the license plate up so we could all read what was on it. It said TYMFLYZ. "It's a vanity plate," he said.

"What's that?" Joanie asked.

"It's when you can get a license plate that says something special about you. Mr. Tyme always had one on his car because he thought his name was so special." He pointed to the letters. "See. This can be read 'Time Flies.'"

"Oh, I see." Joanie touched the letters. "They mean something, like the things we saw in the cryptography exhibit."

"It must be a clue," I said.

Dr. Drafton frowned. "I don't see how this has anything to do with Mr. Tyme's death, but it's strange that he hid it under the desk."

Joanie took it and turned it over. "Look, there's something written on the back."

There were three letters scratched on the back of the metal. "KMC."

"What does that mean?" I asked.

Dr. Drafton just shook his head and looked confused.

"Kathryn Makes Cookies," Joanie said and grinned. She was obviously trying to impress Dr. Drafton with her memory tricks. "It's a mnemonic, a way to remember the letters."

Dr. Drafton's face got real serious and he stared at the license plate. "Whatever it means, girls, we're going to turn it over to the police."

* * *

We were sitting at Dr. Drafton's kitchen table and eating cookies while we waited for Officer Olssen. "Is your first name 'Jolly,' Dr. Drafton?" I asked. I couldn't stand not knowing.

"No. It's just a game Miss Culberson and I play." He gave me that little grin. "Her name is Lillian, but I call her Lilly. My name is Julian, and she calls me Jolly."

Pet names. That sounds serious.

There was a loud banging at the front door, and Dr. Drafton shuffled toward it. I thought he was moving better than before. Officer Olssen marched in and looked really surprised to see Joanie and me.

"Well," he said, "who have we here?"

"We found an important clue to Mr. Tyme's death," Joanie said and gave him a big smile.

Dr. Drafton told him all about how we found the license plate. "Of course, we're not sure if it has anything to do with Mr. Tyme's death, but we thought we should turn it over to you."

Officer Olssen puffed his chest out like he was real important. "I'm certainly glad you did," he said. "I doubt there's a connection, but I'm going to take it downtown and we'll have someone examine it for fingerprints."

"We all touched it, so our fingerprints are on it," Dr. Drafton said.

"We'll take that into consideration," Officer Olssen said. He walked over and looked down at me. "In the meantime, I want to commend you youngsters for your detective work." I thought he was going to pat me on the head, but he didn't. He put a smile on his face that looked real fake. I guessed he was embarrassed because we found something he didn't find.

"Will you tell us if you find out it's a clue?" I asked, trying to look all nice.

"Absolutely. I'll let you know right away. But remember, we don't want to talk about this to anyone else until we get to the bottom of it." Then he took the license plate and hurried out.

Dr. Drafton looked at his watch. "Well, girls, I think we've had a very productive day, but you need to go home before it gets dark." Then he got this really serious look on his face. "What Officer Olssen said is critical. The most important part of detective work is knowing when to keep a secret. We want to be responsible detectives and not tell anybody else about our discovery. Otherwise, we may interfere with the police investigation. Can you keep the secret?"

Joanie and I both nodded. We found the most important clue, and we'd probably get some kind of reward. "We'll keep the secret," I said.

Joanie and I headed back through the middle of campus toward my house, but I couldn't walk. This was too exciting. There should be fireworks and balloons and clowns, and everybody should be hanging out of windows, throwing flowers, but it was so late in the afternoon, there was hardly anybody around. When we got to the middle of the quad, I threw my hands up in the air and danced. I grabbed Joanie's hands and we flew around in a circle until we got so dizzy we fell down. I flopped over on the grass and looked up at the sky. "This is the most exciting day of my life," I said. "We're going to solve the mystery!"

Joanie said she was excited too, but she had to go home or her mother would worry, so she left. I laid on the quad for a long time, letting the idea sink into my insides. The campus was quiet, but I wanted to tell the world. I jumped up and started running around in a circle with my arms spread out like an airplane. "We solved a murder! We solved a murder!" I guess I wasn't looking where I was going because I turned suddenly and ran right into Andrew Bellinger. He grabbed me by the shoulders and looked down at me real angry-like.

"Who solved a murder?"

I gulped, but I wasn't going to let Meanie Bell ruin my day. "I did," I said and stuck my chin up in the air. "I found the license plate that's going to ID the murderer."

"Sure you did." He snorted and walked away.

Chapter Thirty-Nine

DR. SILVA

"Nice building." Kate pulled her car to the curb.

"Gorgeous," Cece said, looking up at the five-story edifice. "I guess he didn't do so badly after getting fired from the university, eh?"

"He wasn't fired. Remember, Reverend Whitefield said he resigned."

"Yeah. After being told he was going to be fired. Same thing." Cece shrugged and shifted in the seat toward Kate. "But Jenny, one of the girls in the play, filled me in on the scandal. She said there was more to it than just having to resign."

Kate tilted her head. "What more?"

"She said Silva's wife left him over the scandal."

"That's not a surprise. It must be hard for a wife to stand by her husband in those circumstances."

Cece nodded. "But Mrs. Silva was the one with the money. A lot of people thought it was because she had donated a bunch of money that Silva was given those important jobs at the university in the first place. Once he got himself in trouble, she kicked him out, and Dr. Silva's lifestyle took a turn for the worse. That's how he ended up here, being a consultant for marketing jobs."

"I was kind of vague when I phoned and asked him to meet with us. I told him it had to do with an issue regarding the university chapel."

Cece arched an eyebrow. "He probably thinks we're going to ask him to set up a campaign to fund something for the chapel."

"Yeah. I hope we can handle this delicately." Kate took a deep breath and opened the car door.

The lobby of the building was fitted with a dark gray carpet sporting a modern motif. A receptionist sat behind a sleek black desk in front of an alcove just to the left as they entered.

She looked up from her laptop as they approached and gave a polite, "Can I help you?"

"I'm Kathryn Frasier. We're here to see Dr. Silva."

"Yes, Ms. Frasier. Dr. Silva is expecting you. His office is on the third floor. Elevators are there." She pointed a manicured finger to her left and turned back to her laptop.

Dr. Silva's office was halfway down the hallway. The man who opened the door was tall and nice-looking, but Kate didn't think he could be called handsome. His features were regular, and his eyes were a light brown behind tortoiseshell glasses.

His clothes looked expensive. Kate guessed the wife could take her money, but not his personal belongings. He wore a Rolex watch and elegant Italian-leather loafers. Kate detected a whiff of expensive cologne.

The office was small, but chic, with a large plexiglass desk set at the end of the room. It looked out over the street in front of the building. They introduced themselves and Dr. Silva offered them seats on a low gray couch situated against the wall. Kate noted his confident baritone voice.

"Cece," he said, "I believe I remember you from a recent stage performance. Weren't you in the *Belleview Revisited* play?"

"Yes, I was. You have a good memory."

"I enjoy the theater. When I was a young man, I had ambitions to be an actor, but a few lackluster performances made me realize I shouldn't quit my day job."

He laughed and Kathryn suddenly felt embarrassed at the situation. Quitting his day job was exactly what she was going to ask him about. Would he be offended?

Cece jumped in. "Dr. Silva, we don't want to take up much of your time. It's just that we've been asked to look into something, and we think you may be able to help us."

"Kathryn told me it had something to do with events at the university chapel," he said. "However, I haven't been there for a long time now. I'm not connected to things on campus."

"We realize that," Kate said. "However, something came up recently that may have to do with you."

"Oh?" His face registered surprise.

"You see, there have been several prayer requests left in the chapel prayer box, and we think one of them refers to you."

"A prayer request that has to do with me?" He displayed a modest grin. "I suppose we can all use prayers."

"Apparently, this note was dropped in the prayer box back around the time that you ... left the university. It said something about the dross being removed from silver."

"What does that have to do with me?"

"We think the note might be a reference to your name."

"I see." He frowned and leaned forward on his desk. "What exactly did the note say?"

Kathryn took a slip of paper out of her purse and handed it to him. "You can see it's a code. We believe the line 'AG - impurity' is a code that translates to removing the dross from the silver. That's a quote from Proverbs."

Silva looked at the paper and turned it over to see if there was anything on the back. "What is the meaning of the line at the bottom that says 'God Remembers'?"

"We're not sure what it means," Kate said.

Silva glanced at the paper again, then refocused on Kate. "It's a bit of a stretch, don't you think, to say this refers to me? It could be a straightforward reference to the metal silver."

"There have been other prayer requests that are similar," Cece said. "They may be a pattern of someone who has a grudge against important university figures."

Silva frowned. "What were the other requests?"

"There was one that seemed to refer to Mr. Tyme's death."

Silva's frown went deeper. "Mr. Tyme?"

"It was similar to this one," Kate said. "It also had some kind of code and was signed 'God Remembers.'"

"We think the same person who had a grudge against you could have had one against Mr. Tyme," Cece said.

"This is a shock." He sat back in his chair. "Mr. Tyme was a friend of mine." Silva's face had gone pale.

"Can you think of anyone who would have a grudge against you?" Kate asked.

"No." Silva took his glasses off and rubbed the bridge of his nose. "I can't think of anyone who would do this." He put his glasses back on. "You said there were other prayer requests. Do you have them?"

"Reverend Whitefield says he remembers another one, but he can't find it."

"I see." Silva said. "Have you told the police about your concerns?"

"Yes," Kate said, "but they've ruled Mr. Tyme's death an accident and they say they won't reopen the investigation unless there's new evidence. They want hard evidence, and they don't think the prayer requests are important."

He shrugged dismissively. "I think the police are right. What happened to Mr. Tyme was terrible, but the police know what they're doing. And I certainly don't harbor any bad feelings toward anyone. There's no need to open old wounds." He looked at his watch and stood, an indication that the meeting was over. "But definitely keep me informed if you find anything else."

* * *

Mel Silva pulled the venetian blinds up on his window that looked out over Madison Street and watched the two women hurry down the sidewalk.

Could that prayer request really have been about his affair with Janelle? Who would have written it? Malone was the obvious choice, since he had gone to the president of the university with the accusations about sexual harassment. But Malone wasn't a religious man. He wouldn't put a slip of paper in a prayer box.

Maybe it was Penterson. He was one of the moral addicts on campus, and it would be just like Malone to have enlisted Penterson to help get rid of him.

Could it have been Tyme? What a disappointment that guy had been. He had tried to cultivate a relationship with the librarian, hoping the church deacon would protect him. But if Tyme had written that one, who wrote the one about Tyme's death?

It doesn't matter now. I'm washing my hands of this place and moving out of state.

But what if those young women manage to get the police involved in Tyme's death again? They might discover that he had asked Tyme to stand by him during the scandal to help him keep his job, but Tyme had refused. They might infer he held a grudge against Tyme, and they'd come around asking questions.

He turned back into the office and sat behind his desk, absent-mindedly adjusting his Armani tie. *The best course of action is just to ensure everybody knows I have no hard feelings toward anyone.*

* * *

Cece opened the passenger door of Kate's car. "I think he's hiding something."

"Really?" Kate asked. "What?" She slipped into the driver's seat.

"I don't know, but he didn't seem sincere to me."

Kate put the key in the ignition and started the car. "Dr. Cassidy said something the other day when I was at her house. She said most people hide behind a verbal suit of armor."

"I agree," Cece said. "And I think Dr. Silva was wearing his today."

Kate's phone pinged, and she pulled it out of her purse. "It's Reverend Whitefield." She felt a surge of energy and gave a thumbs-up to Cece. "He found the missing prayer request."

Chapter Forty

THE KING CLUE

Reverend Whitefield held up a copy of *War and Peace.* "This is where I found it."

"I'm guessing you got that book from Mr. Tyme's apartment?" Kate asked.

"Yes. I vaguely remembered something about the word 'king' in the prayer request, and Mr. Tyme said it must have to do with the Scripture that says, 'In the spring of the year, the time when kings go out to battle.'" He raised his eyebrows. "I guess I'm becoming something of a sleuth myself."

"I'm impressed," Cece said. "And I'm dying to know what you found."

Whitefield opened the book and pulled out a slip of paper. "Here it is." He handed the note to Kate.

```
A KING'S WRATH IS LIKE THE GROWLING OF A LION
KEEP MY COMMANDMENTS 728
GOD REMEMBERS
```

Kate read the first line out loud. "'A king's wrath is like the growling of a lion.'" She looked up at the minister. "Is that a proverb?"

"Yes," he said. "It's the first part of Proverbs 19:12."

Kate read the second line of the prayer request. "'Keep my commandments.' Is that a proverb?"

Whitefield wrinkled his brow. "Those words appear in several places. Proverbs 3, 4, and 7 all contain that phrase. And there are many other places in Scripture."

"And the number seven two eight. Could it be a chapter and verse? Chapter seven, verse twenty-eight?"

The minister shook his head. "I thought of that too, but there is no verse twenty-eight in Proverbs chapter seven."

"Maybe it refers to a specific commandment." Kate turned to her sister. "Cece, didn't Maimonides enumerate the commandments? Could this be commandment number seven hundred and twenty-eight?"

"Maimonides did count the commandments, but he only came up with six hundred and thirteen. This number is way beyond that." Cece took the paper and studied it. "I don't get it."

Kate looked over her sister's shoulder. "It sure fits the pattern, though." She turned to Reverend Whitefield. "Do you know when this one was put in the prayer box?"

"This was the request we found about three months ago in the early spring. Like I said, Mr. Tyme thought it referred to the Bible verse about kings going to war. There was a lot of internal squabbling around that time about the university budget."

"What was happening with the budget?" Kate asked.

"The university budget had been affected by the financial crisis, and some programs were going to have to be cut. It was all over the newspapers, and the faculty was up in arms." He gave a sigh. "Mr. Tyme was caught up in it, too, because the library was having its budget cut. Tyme thought the prayer request must have to do with the internal wars for money."

"So there's a king who's growling. Who would that be?" Cece asked.

Reverend Whitefield put his elbows on the arms of his chair and steepled his fingers together. "I guess the king in that scenario could be the president of the university, Dr. Yarborough. He's the top dog, but he's not the kind of man who gets angry. He's a very diplomatic administrator. Everybody respects him, so I can't see him in that role."

"Could it have been someone else in the administration? How about Dr. Silva?" Kate asked.

"Dr. Silva was known to have a temper, but he was gone by the time this prayer request was left." Whitefield stood and paced behind his desk. "I suppose the king could be one of the department chairs. I've heard people say some of them see themselves as emperors building their own kingdoms."

"But which department chair would this refer to?" Kate asked.

"Good question. There are dozens of departments on campus. Maybe it's just a reference to department chairs in general."

"Or maybe it's referring to a particularly unlikeable department chair," Kate said.

Cece gasped. "Malone. Detective Carlioni said Dr. Malone was not well-liked on campus. He told us a lot of people thought of him as a tyrant."

"That could be it." Reverend Whitefield sank back into his chair. "This prayer request probably came in around the time Dr. Malone was injured."

"Didn't you say this was the request that Mr. Tyme thought he had figured out?" Kate asked.

"Yes. He mentioned the king prayer request when we talked on the phone, but he didn't say anything about Dr. Malone."

"It makes sense, though. Three university employees. Silva was fired, Malone was injured, and Tyme may have been murdered. This clue must refer to Dr. Malone." Kate plunked herself down into one of the chairs. "But what does 'Keep My Commandments' mean?"

Chapter Forty-One

A PROVERB FOR CARLIONI

Carlioni put his head in his hands. "Why can't I get rid of this woman? She's like a bad penny."

MacMillan hung his coat on the hook by the door. "Let me guess. It's Kathryn Frasier."

"She's an albatross around my neck. She won't be happy until she's driven me mad."

"Oh, come on, Carli. She's a great person, and she's trying to help us." He took the phone message Carlioni held out to him. "She's got information on the Malone case?"

"She *says* she has information." Carlioni shook his head. "You know her. She probably overheard something, and she's going to make a big deal about it."

MacMillan stepped back and raised one eyebrow. "I think you're jealous of her."

"Jealous? Of Miss Smarter-than-everybody-else?" He snorted. "I'm a professional detective. She's a snooty amateur, and I'm tired of having to put up with her."

"That isn't fair, Carli. She's smart and she's never acted snooty. I want to hear what she has to say."

There was a knock at the door. Carlioni threw his hands up. "Well, you'll get your chance now. Ten to one, that's her."

MacMillan opened the door. "Well, hi there, Kathryn." He looked around. "Where's your sidekick?"

"You mean Cece? She's at rehearsal for the play she's in." She took a couple of steps into the office. "Is this a good time for us to talk about the Malone case?"

Carlioni uttered an audible groan. "Good as any," he said. "Whatcha got?"

Kathryn handed him a slip of paper.

Carlioni glanced at it and looked up at Kate with sagging eyelids and a tone of skepticism in his voice. "Another prayer request?" He looked back down at the paper and read from it. "'A king's wrath is like the growling of a lion.'" He handed it to MacMillan.

"Yes." Kate bounced up and down on her toes. "Remember we said there were three people who got injured or killed?" She walked to the whiteboard. It had been erased since her last visit, so she picked up a marker and wrote the three names down the left side: Silva, Malone, Tyme.

Next to Silva, she wrote: The Silver Clue. "Remember, the clue referenced the proverb 'Take away the dross from the silver.' That could have to do with Dr. Silva, who was being threatened with being fired for sexual harassment."

Beside Tyme, she wrote: The Coal Clue. "It said something about putting burning coals on someone's head. That certainly happened to Mr. Tyme."

Next to Malone, she wrote: The King Clue. She turned back to Carlioni. "Three people. Each one had some dramatic event happen to them, and there are prayer requests that seem to reference each of them."

"Wait a minute," Carlioni said. He pointed to the whiteboard. "What does a growling king have to do with Dr. Malone?"

"We figure Dr. Malone may be the growling king. Everyone knows him to be an acerbic personality, and there were a lot of arguments about the university budget at that time. Maybe somebody took it all too seriously and decided to get rid of Dr. Malone."

Carlioni took the paper back from MacMillan. "What's this part mean?" He pointed to the paper and read, "'Keep My Commandments 728.'" He looked up at Kate with one eyebrow raised.

"We don't really understand that part of it," she admitted, "but the pattern is the same—a proverb at the top and the words 'God Remembers' at the bottom."

Kate waited as Carlioni leaned back in his chair and worked over his stress ball while he stared at the ceiling. Finally, he stood and walked around his desk. "You've been very helpful." He took her arm and guided her toward the door. "We'll keep the prayer request as evidence." He opened the door. "Thanks very much."

"But Detective Carlioni—" Kathryn said.

"I have another meeting," he replied. "Thanks for stopping by. We'll be in touch."

Carlioni closed the door behind her and turned to his partner.

"That wasn't good, Carli. She has something there."

Carlioni's voice turned matter of fact. "I know she has, and we're going to jump all over this." He stared at the whiteboard with the three names written there. "If we can tie this thing to Dr. Malone's hit-and-run, maybe we can get Simpkins to reopen the Tyme case." He picked up the stress ball and gave it a ferocious squeeze. "Do you have a Bible, Mac? I want to take a look at the Book of Proverbs."

Chapter Forty-Two

DR. MALONE

"I'm not so sure this is a good idea." Cece frowned as she and Kathryn approached the large two-story brick home on the corner of Franklin and Messick.

"I know." Kate rang the doorbell. "But Detective Carlioni didn't think much of the second prayer request, so we're going to have to do some checking ourselves." The door was opened by a petite woman in a nurse's uniform. She looked decidedly harried. "Yes?"

"I'm Kathryn Frasier," Kate said, "and this is my sister, Cece Goldman. I called earlier and asked if we could drop by to talk to Dr. Malone."

"Oh, yes," the nurse answered. Her face relaxed a little. "I was the one you talked to. Come in." She opened the door wide, and they stepped into the front hall. "The doctors say it's all right for Dr. Malone to have visitors as long as they don't upset him." She raised her eyes heavenward. "Although Dr. Malone seems to be in a perpetual state of upset."

"We could come back another time if you prefer," Cece said and stepped back toward the door.

"No, no. This is as good a time as any." She leaned in toward them and lowered her voice to a near whisper. "I just warn you, he's been especially rabid today. More than usual. But you'll see for yourselves."

She motioned them to follow her. Kate and Cece glanced at each other, and Cece raised her eyebrows as the nurse led them up the stairs.

As they reached the landing, Kate heard a buzzing, and the nurse pulled a device out of her pocket. Before she could respond, a raspy voice shouted from a room at the end of the hall, "Nurse! Nurse!"

The nurse picked up her pace. "Coming," she called out.

As they got to the doorway of the bedroom, Kate saw a man sitting in a large chair next to an empty hospital bed. There was a walker next to his chair. He had a long, rectangular face that was blotchy red. A beaked nose jutted out aggressively under small, dark eyes that darted back and forth, reminding Kate of a hawk or an eagle. Definitely a predator.

As soon as they stepped in the room, Dr. Malone barked at the nurse, "There you are. Where have you been, woman? Didn't you get the page I sent you?"

"Yes, Dr. Malone." The nurse took little geisha steps toward the chair, her rubber-soled shoes making soft chirping noises with each step on the hardwood floor. "I just saw the page, but I was at the front door. These are the ladies I told you about."

"Yes, yes." He waved Kathryn and Cece toward chairs opposite him. "Nurse, I need ice in this water. You know I can't stand drinking room-temperature liquid." He picked up a cup from the side table and held it out without making eye contact with the nurse.

Watching the nurse as she took the cup from the man's hand, Kathryn thought how nice it was to work with computers. Whatever the frustrations might be, at least they didn't yell.

"I'll bring you a fresh cup of water with ice right away." The nurse turned and left the room.

Malone adjusted his position in the chair. "Hard to get decent help these days." He leveled his eyes at Kathryn. "You want to talk about the accident?" Before she could respond, he waved his hand. "Police are totally incompetent. How hard can it be to find the car that ran into me? It must have dents or a broken headlight or something. But they claim they haven't found anything." He made a throaty sound that Kate took for a growl.

"Dr. Malone, do you think the driver could have driven into you on purpose?"

Malone rolled his eyes. "Well now there's an obvious statement if I ever heard one. I've done a lot for this university, young lady. I've been very successful, and the place is full of jealous little laggards who would like nothing better than to bump me off."

"Like who?" Cece asked.

"Like anybody who would benefit from my demise. I gave the police a whole list of possibilities. Look at Penterson. He's practically drooling at the chance to become chairman. And Bellinger's the type to hold a grudge because I wouldn't sign off on his tenure request." He shook his head. "Get the list from the police if you want to know."

Kathryn leaned toward him. "The police told us you were riding your bicycle after dark in the rain. Wasn't that dangerous?"

Malone's face reddened and he coughed. "I had to stay late at work that night. My bicycle was the only mode of transportation home. I didn't have a choice."

Kate took a piece of paper out of her purse. "Dr. Malone, we found a note that may have something to do with your accident."

Malone's visage changed from a charging bull to a stag sniffing the air, aware of a shift in the wind. "A note?" he said.

She handed it to him.

He took his glasses from the side table and adjusted them on his nose with a scowl. The room was completely silent as he reviewed the contents and then looked up, his eyes focusing on something beyond the room. She could sense his mind tracing possible paths to explain the note.

"Here's your ice water." The nurse returned and placed the cup on the side table. "Anything else?"

"No. Not now." His voice reflected a simple statement, not a command, and the nurse looked a little taken aback by it. She glanced at Kathryn and Cece as if to ask what had brought about this remarkable change. "You can go," he said without emotion.

After the nurse left, Malone held the paper up. "Where did you get this?"

"It's a copy of a note that was left in the prayer box at the chapel," Kate replied.

"And why do you think it has anything to do with me or my accident?"

Kate explained. "We believe it was left in the prayer box around the time of your accident, and it's similar to others that were left there. Each one starts with a proverb and ends with the words 'God Remembers.'"

He grew silent, and Kate could sense the wheels turning. Finally, he looked up. "I don't see the logic in it. I'm not a religious man. Why would someone leave a prayer request that has to do with me?"

"We believe there may be a pattern," Kate said. "There were three prayer requests left in the prayer box over the last six months or so. Each one seems to have something to do with a major event on campus."

"What were the others?"

"The last one seems to be a reference to Mr. Tyme," Kate said.

"Tyme?" Malone's voice boomed out. "That little do-nothing? What a sorry excuse for a librarian. Spent all his time doing crossword puzzles and not modernizing the place. I'm not surprised he was careless enough to catch himself on fire."

"We were wondering if someone who wanted to hurt you may have also wanted to hurt Mr. Tyme," Kate said.

Malone let the paper drop onto his lap. "Tyme and I are not in the same category," he said. "A lot of people would want my job, but I can't imagine anybody wanting his." He took a sip from his newly iced cup of water. "Maybe somebody who wants a promotion in the library. But that doesn't have anything to do with me."

"How about Dr. Silva?" Cece asked.

"Silva?" Malone looked up with a startled expression. "What does he have to do with this?"

"There's another note that seems to refer to Dr. Silva. It also has the words 'God Remembers' at the bottom."

Malone shook his head again. "I can't believe I would be lumped in with him," he said. "Silva was a smooth operator all right. He had a knack for securing grant money, but he was a mediocre computer scientist. The only reason he got the job in the first place was because of his wife's money. She was a big donor and made demands on the administrators. But under his leadership, the department slipped in the national rankings, so they promoted him to chancellor and made me chairman. It was a good decision all around."

He took another swig of ice water and replaced the cup on the night table with a thud. "Of course, Silva couldn't keep his hands off the women in the chancellor's office, and rumors were all over campus. I heard some students talking about it out on the quad one day with the gardener right there within earshot. What's worse, the press was beginning to get wind of it. I personally talked to the president and suggested the retirement package. The sendoff wasn't great, but it avoided a scandal."

"Why did you get involved?" Cece asked.

"Anything that damages the reputation of the university is bad for me and my department." The red crept back into his face. "Besides, one of the girls Silva was lusting after is the daughter of a friend of mine. It was my duty to my friend to put a stop to it."

"Who is she?" Kate asked.

"Her name is Janelle. Janelle Kaiser."

* * *

Leon Malone leaned back on his cushioned headrest and listened to the women's footsteps fade as they left the house.

He felt the old anger bubbling up again as he recalled the events surrounding Silva's resignation. Serving on the university oversight committee had given Malone access to all the emails that went through university servers. It wasn't his fault Silva had been a fool and sent that one explicit email to Janelle that nailed his fate. It was part of Malone's responsibility to protect the university, and he had taken a copy of the email to the president of the university as soon as he saw it.

Janelle's father, Brian Kaiser, was a good friend, and he had been very grateful to get his daughter out of Silva's clutches. President Yarborough had sworn he would never reveal Malone's role in supplying the evidence for Silva's resignation. But suppose Yarborough had let the information slip? Why would somebody write a prayer request about it?

He thought back to the day of the accident. He had received a call from a journalist who wanted to do a story about his work at the university. The guy had said his flight would land around seven in the evening, and they had agreed to meet at eight o'clock in Malone's office. When he hadn't shown up by nine o'clock, Malone had called the number the reporter had called from. He didn't answer, and there was no voice mail message.

Malone shifted his weight and clamped his teeth together hard. It wasn't the pain in his legs. It was knowing someone had gotten the best of him. All his life, he'd been in charge. And then he fell for an idiotic prank a ten-year-old kid would have spotted. He imagined a gaggle of undergraduates watching from the bushes and waiting to see how long it would take him to figure it out.

When the police asked why he was so late going home that night, he had told them he had some work to catch up on. No one could ever find out he'd been taken for a fool.

But now it looked like someone had impersonated a reporter to keep him at the university after dark. The prayer request Kathryn Frasier showed him could be a clue. Could someone have been targeting him?

He closed his eyes and tried to recall every moment of that night. With the rain and his anger about the fake journalist, he hadn't heard the car until it was right on him. Surely he would have seen the light from the car's headlights if they had been on. Did the driver turn them off on purpose? The sound of the gravel crunching under the car's tires had startled him, and a bright flash of lightning had illuminated the sky. He had turned his head to the left to be sure he was out of the way, and then everything seemed to explode and he was falling. Then nothing until he woke up in the hospital.

He replayed it in his mind again and again. Did his brain record anything about the driver of the car? He turned his head to the left, trying to remember. The lightning had provided enough light to see inside the car. Had he seen who was behind the wheel? Was it a dream, or did he remember red hair?

* * *

"So, what do you think about Dr. Malone?" Kate asked Cece as they walked back toward campus.

Cece stopped on the sidewalk and crossed her arms. "He's hiding something."

"Do you really think so?" Kate stopped and turned to her sister. "I thought he was very forthcoming."

Cece reached out and put her hand on Kate's shoulder. "You know, sister, you're a brilliant woman. I think you can solve any problem in the world." She tilted her head and put a pained look on her face. "But you're a little naive when it comes to people."

"Naive? Me?"

"Yes." Cece planted her hands on her hips. "Didn't you notice how defensive he got when you asked him about why he was riding his bike at night in the rain?"

"I thought he was just embarrassed."

"I think there's something Dr. Malone doesn't want us to know."

Kate bent from the waist. "I bow to your superior intuition. You are the expert on all things human." She straightened up and started walking again. "Everybody seems to be hiding something, but I feel like the truth is right in front of us. If we could only solve that code, maybe we would see it."

"You know what they say," Cece said as she fell in beside Kate. "With time, all things are revealed."

Kate nodded. "I just hope we can uncover the truth before somebody else gets hurt."

Chapter Forty-Three

ANDREW'S FOLLY

Kate strolled across campus toward the rectory, taking her time to decide how to relay her meeting with Dr. Malone to Reverend Whitefield.

"Still playing hooky from your job?" A male voice came from behind her, and she wheeled around. Andrew Bellinger strode through the quad toward her. He was wearing a gray T-shirt over sweatpants and carried a gym bag over his shoulder. His T-shirt strained over impressive biceps.

Kate stopped and waited for him to catch up. "Hi, Andrew. Are you coming from the gym?"

"Very perceptive," he said as he came alongside. "I have to keep my strength up. Never know when I may have to wrestle a differential equation to the ground."

Kate looked up into his face and smiled. So, Andrew Bellinger had a sense of humor after all.

He shifted the gym bag to the other shoulder as they walked together. "Getting anywhere with your codes?"

"I've made a little progress, but I haven't talked to Miss Ramen for a while."

"Miss Ramen seems like a strange bird." He ran a hand through his damp hair. "A real anachronism."

"Why do you say that?"

"Didn't you see her? She looks like a fossil from the early 1900s. Her time is way past, sort of like that." He pointed toward the bell tower.

"The bell tower?"

"No, the clock."

"I love that clock," Kate said. "Did you know the chimes are exactly in the key of C-sharp?"

"Never heard that before," he said. "Are you an expert on the bell tower clock?"

"I learned a few things about it recently."

"Like?"

"It was given to the university by a wealthy philanthropist. Mr. Tyme, the librarian, arranged for the donation, and like I told you before, he was in charge of the maintenance of the clock until he died." She noticed the worry line deepen between Andrew's brows. Did the mention of Mr. Tyme have that effect?

"It's an unnecessary anachronism," he grunted.

Kate decided to push it. "Mr. Tyme didn't think so."

"Mr. Tyme wanted to keep a nineteenth-century mechanism working when it would have been simpler and cheaper to install one with an electric motor." He snorted. "And he made a big deal about it being associated with the church. I guess it made him feel important because he was some kind of official at the chapel."

"What's wrong with it being associated with the church?"

"Think about it, Kathryn. Religious faith has no place on a university campus. It's the very antithesis of what we're doing here."

Kate turned to face him and crossed her arms. "I don't get it. Why are the two things opposite?"

Andrew pointed to a bench, and she sat. He dropped the gym bag on the ground and stood in front of her like a class lecturer. "Look at it this way. Faith is all about believing somebody else is in charge. You just close your eyes and hope for the best." He put his foot up on the bench and made a wide, sweeping gesture with his arm. "But the university is about learning. It's about uncovering the truths of the universe. It's about mankind taking charge of his own destiny."

"I don't think faith is a question of closing one's eyes to truth. In fact,

I think God wants us to understand his universe. He wants us to learn." She paused and tried to remember. "Isn't there a proverb in the Bible that says something like 'It's the pleasure of God to conceal things and the pleasure of kings to find them out.'?"

"I never heard that one."

"Maybe you should read the Book of Proverbs. There's a lot of wisdom in it."

He shook his head. "That's what my religious friends tell me. They say there's wisdom in the Bible." He looked down at her. His face was so close she could see the little drops of perspiration and smell his aftershave. Ralph Lauren.

He continued, "But we shouldn't be concerned with words from an ancient book. We should be dealing with facts. It's the only way to move civilization forward. All the mumbo jumbo in the world isn't going to solve the problems we have in society."

"And you think universities are the solution?"

"I believe putting the scientific method to work in the world at large will solve our problems. When everyone sees that the only way we can live is through science, we'll have a much more realistic world." He grinned in triumph. "I heard your father give a talk once about Aristotle. He said Aristotle was considered the first great scientist."

"That's true." Kate grinned back at him. She was getting ready to turn his argument on its head and found an almost giddy excitement welling up. "My father admired Aristotle because he tried to understand the universe."

"Exactly my point," Andrew said.

"But Dad also told me almost everything Aristotle concluded about the universe was wrong!" She paused and watched the color rise in Andrew's face. "Aristotle didn't understand gravity. He thought when you dropped something, it would have the same velocity until it hit the ground. He had lots of misconceptions."

"Yes, but other scientists came along and moved our understanding forward."

"Right, but that doesn't mean any of them had absolute truth." Kate felt her face grow warm. "Although you seem to think you've found it."

"I didn't say that."

"It seems to me that it's a worthy goal to keep trying to understand the truth in the universe, but it's arrogant to assume we can gain one hundred percent truth. Remember, Einstein said, 'Nature shows us only the tail of the lion.' I think he was telling us to remain humble about what we know while we try to discover more about ourselves and our environment."

"Humility? On a university campus? That's a good one." Andrew laughed. "We hold the highest calling on the planet. Why should we be humble?"

"Because you don't know everything. We need to temper our acquisition of knowledge with the humility to learn how to use it. You may think you understand some new truth, but you need to be aware of your own inadequacies."

Just at that moment, the bell tower clock chimed.

Andrew looked at his watch. "Your anachronism just reminded me that I have to meet with some remedial students in a few minutes. There's a small chance I can get them to open their eyes and think." He took his foot off the bench and picked up his gym bag. "Maybe we can continue this conversation later." He turned and walked away.

* * *

Andrew strode across campus toward the computer science building, his footsteps keeping time with his heartbeat. His chance meeting with Kathryn Frasier had energized him. She was the most interesting woman he had met in a long time. Good mind inside a great body.

Their debate had been fun. She stood her ground, and he liked that. Maybe she even won this round. *I'll have to ask for a rematch.* A steamy grin slid across his face.

As he reached the door of the building, his smile faded and he hesitated. That was the second time she had brought up Mr. Tyme's name to him. *She must know something. But how could she?*

He pulled the door open, took the stairs two at a time, and walked briskly down the hall toward his office. There were two students waiting outside.

"I don't have time for office hours now," he said. "Something's come up."

Johnny Dembrowski shrugged. "I'll come back later."

But Celeste Poindexter persisted. "I just have a quick question about the Computers for Artists course."

"Not now." His voice was louder and harsher than he intended, but never mind. He pushed by her, unlocked the door, and walked into the room. Then he closed the door firmly behind him.

He sat behind his desk, automatically opened his laptop to the class notes folder, and stared at the contents. But he couldn't focus.

He took a deep breath. *How much does Kathryn Frasier know about Mr. Tyme?*

Why had he ever trusted that man? Andrew sat back and tried to recall the exact conversation they'd had. When was it? A couple of months ago. He had admitted to Mr. Tyme the mistake he had made as an undergrad. Stealing a copy of the final exam almost got him kicked out of school. He had stolen it from the office files when the secretary wasn't looking and sold it to the student who had asked him to get it. When that mediocre student made a perfect score on the final, everybody knew something was wrong.

That rotten louse had admitted cheating and had fingered him, but they couldn't prove anything, and he denied stealing the exam. The other student got kicked out, but Andrew had never felt guilty about it. At least not until he went to church with one of his girlfriends and heard Reverend Whitefield talk about sin.

Andrew put his head in his hands. *I'm not a sinner. I've worked hard for everything I've gotten. It's not my fault that stupid guy paid me. He was the one who cheated. Not me.*

Mr. Tyme had seemed so concerned when he asked to talk to him. Like a good friend. He hadn't experienced many close friendships in life. A foster family upbringing didn't exactly prepare him for strong relationships. But Mr. Tyme had reached out to him as if he really cared. How stupid he'd been to confide in him.

Then there was that Friday when he talked to Mr. Tyme again in the library. He tried to explain to Tyme how important it was to keep the secret, but Tyme had been nervous and distracted. He might have been planning to take Andrew's confession to the administration. Tyme was the one person who could have gotten Andrew fired.

But thankfully, that was no longer possible. Tyme was dead, and he took with him the dirty secret that could tank Andrew's career.

But could he have told someone? He said he would never share the information, but maybe he was like all the others. The way Kathryn Frasier seemed so interested in Mr. Tyme might mean she knew something. Had Tyme ratted on him?

He'd have to find out.

Chapter Forty-Four

ANDREW HAS A PLAN

Andrew closed the file with the class notes and opened his email. A long list of subjects filled the screen, but one name jumped out at him. Silva.

He remembered now. Silva and Tyme had been pretty chummy. He had seen them having lunch in the faculty dining room. Silva had been friends with a lot of the staff once he got to be chancellor. Rumor was he wanted to be president of the university. But he had a lot of enemies too, and one of them had made a stink about Silva's dalliance with Janelle, and that did him in. Was it Tyme who had ratted him out?

In his position as chancellor, Silva would have known whether Tyme had spilled the beans about Andrew's past to the upper administrators. Would he be willing to tell? Silva must be angry at the administration for the way they had treated him. He'd know if there was a black mark that would keep a faculty member from advancing.

Andrew read through Silva's email. It said he was soliciting funds for some project he was pushing. Andrew sat back in his chair and rubbed his hands together while the plan developed in his mind. Then he picked up his phone and punched the number at the bottom of Silva's email. Silva himself picked up.

"Andrew, hello. Nice of you to call." Silva's voice had the same tone of pleasant authority he remembered. When Silva was at the university,

Andrew had considered him to be a fluff ball—high on image, low on brains. But he was a political animal, and Andrew would have to be careful not to overplay his hand.

"Good afternoon, Chancellor. I'm glad I was able to reach you." Andrew felt a drop of sweat slide down the side of his face, and he brushed it away. "I just read your email about the education project you're soliciting help for, and I think it might be something I'd like to support."

"Wonderful. Glad to hear it. I can send you some additional information if you like and we can discuss how you can get involved. We're always looking for good faculty members to spread the word, and of course we appreciate any financial support we can get." Andrew could hear papers being shuffled on the other end of the line and knew Silva didn't consider him important enough to extend the conversation.

He forced his voice to match Silva's confident tone. "I definitely want to add my support. Send me whatever information you have." Andrew paused. He had to come across with the right tone. Not prying. Just interested. "One question, though. Wasn't Mr. Tyme involved in that organization a while back?" he asked.

"Mr. Tyme?" The paper shuffling stopped.

"Yes. You remember him. He was the librarian who died in a fire a few weeks ago."

"Yes, I knew him, but I wasn't aware Tyme was ever involved in this project," Silva replied. "Why do you ask?"

"No reason. It's just that I heard some rumors about Mr. Tyme that kind of turned me off anything he supported."

"What rumors?" Silva's voice lost its authoritative tone. He sounded very curious.

"Like he was not a friend of the faculty. Using his position as a deacon to get private information out of people that he used against them. Things like that."

"I never heard that." Silva sounded cautious.

"So he never came to you with any nasty rumors about faculty members?" Andrew tried to make his voice sound surprised.

"No. Not at all. Andrew, you can rest assured this venture is completely aboveboard, and Mr. Tyme had nothing to do with it." Silva's voice returned to a firm, matter-of-fact tone.

"Well, that's a relief." *You can't imagine what a relief.* "Too bad the old guy died. I figured maybe he pried into other people's business so much he really was murdered, like that Penterson girl keeps saying."

"Murdered?" Andrew heard Silva take a noisy breath. "The police ruled his death an accident."

"I guess that's right, but Nate Penterson's daughter is running around campus saying Mr. Tyme was murdered, and she's solving the crime."

"I didn't know Penterson had a daughter."

"He does. That stupid carrot-top." He'd heard Silva had a bad opinion of Dr. Penterson, so calling him a stupid carrot-top should score some points. "The daughter is nine or ten years old and completely out of control. She claims she found a license plate that will solve a crime."

"I see." There was a pause. Then Silva cleared his throat. "You know children. They're always coming up with some silly notion."

"Penterson's daughter seems to have more than her share of nonsense. And you should see her. She looks like a hobo, always wearing overalls and a T-shirt."

"Sounds like she needs some oversight."

Andrew laughed casually. "She won't get it from her father. Penterson can't even oversee the department. You won't believe this, but he's probably even worse than old Malone." More brownie points. Dissing Malone might ingratiate him even more to Silva. "Ever since you left, the department has gone downhill."

"I didn't think Penterson had it in him, but sometimes people rise to the occasion. Of course, Malone was a lost cause from day one. Arrogant know-it-all." Another pause, then a change in tone. "But nobody deserves to be hurt the way he was in that terrible accident. How is he doing? Have you seen him lately?"

"I hear he's confined to his home with multiple injuries, but he's just too mean to die."

"Do the police know any more about the accident?"

"I hear they've given up. They think it must have been somebody from out of the area, since they can't find a car around with any damage on it. They've gone through just about every car in Bellevue."

"I know. They came around to check my car even, though I was out of the state when it happened. At least they did a thorough job. They'll probably put it in the cold case file so they can do something more important, like arresting people for jaywalking on Madison Street."

Andrew laughed heartily. "The Bellevue police aren't the sharpest tools in the shed."

Silva chuckled in return. "Exactly. Well, Andrew, it was great to speak with you. I have another meeting now, but I'll have those materials sent out to you right away. Thanks again for your interest."

"Thank you, Chancellor, for the opportunity to get in on the ground floor of a good cause." Andrew hung up and leaned back in his chair. He felt the moisture under his armpits, but no matter. If there had been anything in the university files about his own past indiscretions that could hurt him, Silva would have given some indication. Unfortunate that he had to badmouth so many people in order to get the information, but you do what you have to do to protect yourself.

Andrew hummed a tune as he deleted Silva's email.

Chapter Forty-Five

THE MINISTER AND THE PSYCHOLOGIST

"It's nice of you to drop by." Reverend Whitefield settled back in his desk chair and gestured for his visitor to take the seat across from him in his study. "I haven't seen you at services in quite a while." He tried to thread the needle between inquiring after circumstances and implying guilt.

The man shrugged. "You know how things are. Martha was always the devout one in the family. After she died, I became somewhat lax in my spiritual life."

"I understand." Whitefield nodded and smiled. "It's not uncommon, but I'm happy to see you here now. You said on the phone you had something important to talk about."

The visitor sat forward in the straight chair. He wore a blue dress shirt over khaki slacks. His herringbone jacket that was frayed at the cuffs and his slightly ruffled hair gave him the appearance of a venerable university professor.

"I feel a little foolish," he said. "I'm usually quite confident in my interactions with others, but something happened recently that's been bothering me, and I want to discuss it with you."

"Of course. I'm happy to listen. Jan's out for the day doing some home visits, but I make a tolerable cup of coffee if you'd like one." He pointed to a coffee maker on the credenza next to his desk.

"Yes, thanks. It smells wonderful."

"It's French roast. I just made it a few minutes ago." Whitefield filled a cup and offered cream and sugar. "Now, Julian, please tell me what's on your mind."

Dr. Drafton took a sip of coffee. "Several days ago, two young girls came to visit me. You probably know them—Irene Penterson and her cousin, Joanie."

"Yes, I know the children."

"I've known Irene since she was a baby. Her mother was a distant relative, and Nate brings her by occasionally to say hello."

Drafton took another sip of coffee and placed the cup on the desk. His eyes brightened. "When I answered the doorbell, I was surprised to see the two young girls there. Irene said they wanted to interview me about university buildings, but I could tell that was just an excuse for something else. You may remember my academic specialty was childhood psychology, so I was delighted to have the chance to talk to them to see what they were really up to."

"Ah. So they became experimental subjects."

Drafton made a gentle shrug. "I suppose you could say that. But to be honest, they were so bright and genuine that I found myself enjoying their company, and I was curious to find out what their motivation was."

"Let me guess," Whitefield said. "They wanted you to help them investigate Mr. Tyme's death."

Drafton raised his eyebrows in surprise. "I'm impressed with your knowledge, Jim. How did you know?"

"Someone told me Irene had overheard a conversation that she took to mean Mr. Tyme had been murdered, and she decided she wanted to solve the crime." He shook his head. "I've also known Reen for most of her life, and I wasn't surprised to hear that she would cast herself as a twenty-first-century Nancy Drew. But I am surprised to hear she's kept up with it this long and she wanted you to help them."

"When I heard their story about Mr. Tyme, I realized they had formulated a murder in their minds, and I thought I could help dispel their misconceptions."

"How were you going to do that?"

"By joining their team of murder investigators. Children are often told what to believe by adults, when they would prefer to figure it out for themselves, so rather than telling them they were wrong, I decided to show them by taking them to Mr. Tyme's office and having them search for clues. I knew the police had done their own investigation, so I was confident we wouldn't find anything, and the children would realize they were wrong."

"Sounds like an excellent plan," Whitefield said.

"It was a good plan. Unfortunately, it didn't work out the way I hoped." He took another sip of coffee and frowned. "The girls found something in the office that they immediately decided was a clue."

Reverend Whitefield sat upright in his chair, and the smile dropped off his face. "What did they find?"

"It was an automobile license plate hidden under the desk in the office. It was just a vanity license plate spelling out TYMFLYZ, but it was such a surprise that I'm afraid it only confirmed their suspicions that Mr. Tyme had been murdered."

Reverend Whitefield sat for several seconds, trying to put this new piece of the puzzle in place. "What did you do with the license plate?" he asked.

"I turned it over to the police. Although I don't see how it could have anything to do with Mr. Tyme's death, I can't stop thinking about it. That's why I came to see you."

Reverend Whitefield raised his eyebrows as a signal to go on.

"I called the police department today and talked to Officer Olssen. He's the one who took the license plate back to police headquarters. He said they were looking into it, but didn't think it had anything to do with Mr. Tyme's death. But then he mentioned you."

"Me?"

"He said you also had some concerns about Mr. Tyme's death and wanted to know if we were working together. I thought we should talk."

The minister leaned his forearms on his desk as he spoke. "What Officer Olssen told you is true. I did have some concerns about Mr. Tyme's death. Although I have no idea what an automobile license plate could have to do with anything, I'm convinced there may have been foul play." Whitefield filled Dr. Drafton in on the prayer request that seemed to refer to Mr. Tyme. "But no matter what happened to Mr. Tyme, I'm more worried about the children."

"That is my concern as well," Drafton said. "If there is a danger, I don't want anyone to know the young girls are involved. I told the girls they shouldn't say anything to anyone about what we found until I tell them it's all right. I told them keeping this secret may be the most important part of detective work."

"Great idea. Do you think they'll do it?"

"I think so. I called Nate Penterson last night. He said he had an idea of something else to keep the children occupied. He found someone to take them to the theater."

Chapter Forty-Six

JOANIE GETS A PART

"I've never been backstage before," Reen said as she and Joanie followed Kathryn behind the curtain at the University Theater stage. "It looks different back here."

"It's pretty here." Joanie ran her hand down the dark red, velvet curtain and smiled at Kate. "Where's Cece?"

"She'll meet us here soon. The director wanted to talk to her for a minute."

Cece walked offstage and waved. "Hi, ladies. Glad you could make it."

Joanie ran to Cece. "I saw you on the stage. You were wonderful."

Reen was looking behind every screen she could find. "Wow. This place is big."

"Come on." Cece led them to a dressing room at the far end of the theater. "I'll just change clothes and we can go outside." She took off the powdered wig she was wearing and stepped behind a partition. "Did you like the rehearsal?" she called out.

"Yes!" Joanie's eyes were wide with excitement. "I loved it. You looked so beautiful, and that man is so handsome."

"You must mean Reggie. Everybody thinks he's a hunk. What did you think of his acting ability?"

"I don't know," Joanie replied. "It just made me feel bumpy all over when he kissed you." She sat on the stool in front of the brightly lit mirror and sighed. "That was so romantic."

Cece picked up a hairbrush from her vanity and swiped at her hair. "Well, I hope the critics are as kind as you are, cutie." She chucked Joanie under the chin. "Let's go. I'll take you to the wardrobe room and then I'll introduce you to the rest of the cast."

When they left the dressing room, they encountered several of the actors roaming around backstage in various forms of dress. Some had taken off their wigs and jackets. Kate thought it looked like an eighteenth-century aristocratic party gone bad.

Cece opened the door to the wardrobe room and motioned them in. The room was full of racks of costumes and shelves full of wigs and props. She led her visitors around, pointing out the hats for the Revolutionary War play they were planning next year.

Reen tried on a pirate hat and admired herself in the mirror.

Joanie went to the clothes rack. "We could play dress-up here, Reen," she said as she ran her hand along the colorful dresses and shawls. When she got close to the end, she screamed and ran to Cece. "It's a snake!" She pointed to the end of the clothes rack where a long, black snake was hanging.

Cece laughed and picked up the rubber reptile. "It's a fake," she said. "They used it in a play a while back." She handed it to Joanie.

"Ew." Joanie wrinkled her nose and handed it back to Cece. "I hate snakes."

Cece rehung the snake on the clothes rack and pointed to the door. "Come on. I'll introduce you to some of the cast." She raised her eyebrows at Joanie. "Including Reggie."

They left the wardrobe room and sauntered around the backstage area. Cece introduced them to several of the actors and then gestured toward two men standing in the wings. "There's our director, Alan," Cece said. "And that's Reggie talking to him."

"Hey, guys." Cece approached them. "What's up?"

"Hello, Queen Cece," Alan said.

Reggie did a theatrical bow. "Did you bring us some adoring fans?"

Cece chuckled. "This is my sister, Kathryn. And these two young ladies are Reen and Joanie. They sat through the whole rehearsal."

"And who did you like best?" Reggie asked.

"I liked you and Cece the best," Joanie said and blushed.

Reggie took her hand and put it to his lips. "You have fine taste," he said and winked at her.

Joanie's blush turned deep purple.

Reggie looked at his watch. "Oops. Gotta run. Hot date."

Joanie sighed and gazed after Reggie as he walked away.

Alan smiled down at the girls. "I'm glad you liked the performance." He turned to Reen. "What was your favorite part?"

"I liked the fight scene," she said. "Were those real swords?"

"No. We don't use real weapons here. But they look pretty authentic, don't they?"

"What happened to Simone?" Cece asked. "Why did we skip her scene today?" She looked at Reen and Joanie. "Simone is a girl about your age, Joanie. She has a small part, but she wasn't here today."

"Her mother called to say she's sick," Alan said. He shook his head. "I need a stand-in for her so we can get a sense of the timing of the scene." He looked at the youngsters. "You don't happen to know any little girls who might want to help us out in the next few days, do you?"

"I will. I will." Joanie jumped up and down. "I want to help."

"No, Joanie. Remember, you're my assistant." Reen puffed her face up.

"It would just be for a few days until Simone gets back." Alan patted Joanie on her head. "If it's all right with your parents, you can come to rehearsals with Cece."

"Oh, goodie. Cece, is it all right with you?"

"Yes. Of course. You'll be my young actress friend for a few days."

Chapter Forty-Seven

A HASTY TEMPER

Nate leaned back in his office chair and checked his watch. Almost eight o'clock. Reen would be coming in any minute carrying a game of Big Boggle or Scrabble or Clue.

Having a bright child was a challenge. Especially when there was no mother. Nate had thought maybe he should marry again, but it seemed crazy to consider marrying just to provide his child with a mother. He was too busy to be a good husband and besides, there wasn't anyone he'd met who interested him. Not like Trish. He sighed and leaned back.

Reen had been quiet during dinner. Unusual for her. *I hope she isn't getting interested in boys. I hate to think my time with my little girl is almost over.*

Reen appeared at his office door, but instead of bounding in with a game in hand, she walked in empty-handed, slowly crossed the floor, and sagged into the chair opposite his desk.

"What? No game?" Nate pretended to look shocked. "I was sure you'd want to cream me at Risk tonight."

"I don't feel like playing a game." Reen stared at the floor with her bottom lip poking out.

"Do you feel like talking?"

"No."

"Maybe you're coming down with something. Come here and let me feel your forehead."

"I'm not sick, Dad. I feel fine." She didn't move from her chair.

"Hmm. In that case, I suggest we play our game of proverbs." He reached into the desk drawer and pulled out the Proverbs card deck.

"It isn't Wednesday," she said.

"I'm changing the rules," he said. "Proverbs are good every day of the week, so we'll just have an extra dose of wisdom tonight." While he shuffled the cards, he examined his daughter's face. What could be going on inside her head? It must have to do with Joanie. When he had praised the little redhead during dinner for getting a part in the play, Reen had looked away.

"I guess Joanie must be pretty happy about getting a part in Cece's play, huh? That's exciting."

"I guess." Reen looked down at her hands. "But she's going to be spending all her time with them now. She thinks it's the most important thing in her life."

Ah. So that's it. "It's sort of like the time your teacher got you to help her with the science fair, right? You didn't have any time for Joanie."

"It's not like that at all." She looked up with a frown. "Joanie and I had a pact. We said we would play together all summer."

"Things change sometimes, honey. We can't always get our own way."

She clamped her lips together.

Nate fanned the cards out, face down, and held them out. "Pick a proverb, young lady."

Reen indifferently pulled one of the cards from the deck and held it out to him. He took it from her and examined it. It was Proverbs 22:6. Nate stared at the card and said a silent prayer. *Lord, forgive me. I'm going to lie to my child.*

"This is an interesting one," he said. "We haven't seen this one for a long time." He peered up at her over his glasses. "Proverbs 14:29."

Reen's head snapped up. "I don't remember."

"I'll give you a hint. It starts out, 'Whoever is slow to anger.'" He paused, but Reen just stared blankly at him. "Okay. I'll give it to you. 'Whoever is slow to anger has great understanding, but he who has a hasty temper exalts folly.'" He paused again, but Reen dropped her head and didn't say anything.

"Well, I think that's the first time you forgot one. Do you know what this means?"

"I guess it means anger is bad." Her chin quivered. "And I have a hasty temper, so I must be bad."

"Come here, honey." He led her over to the couch and they sat next to each other. He gently lifted her chin so that she looked at him. "You're not bad, Reen. Everybody gets angry at one time or another."

Reen's face reddened. "I never saw you get angry, Dad."

"But I have been angry, Reen. Many times."

"Really? But you're a nice person. Nice people don't get mad."

"Of course they do, Reen. When I was in the fifth grade, Jimmy Bladdenburg won the school math contest, and I was so mad I wouldn't even talk to him for a week. I was angry because he was smarter than I was, but I didn't want to admit it."

Reen leaned her hands on her legs. "You didn't like it because he won?"

"That's right. And there were other times when people got promoted to a position I wanted, and it made me mad. But this is one of the things God wants us to correct in our lives."

"How do you correct it?"

"Confess to God that you have these feelings and try to be happy for the other person. God will help you."

"But suppose I'm still mad?"

"Why don't you look around for another friend to play with during the time Joanie is gone?"

Reen bit on her bottom lip. "Most of the kids have gone to camp or gone on vacation with their parents."

There was a silence while he worked on a plan in his mind. "I heard Kathryn Frasier say something about a program for kids to get them into running. You'd be a great runner. Why don't I give her a call and see what this program is?"

Reen sighed. "All right, Dad. I'll give it a try if you want me to."

"That's my girl!" Nate gave a big smile. "We Pentersons don't give up easily. We're like the Energizer Bunny." He pumped his fist in the air. "We just keep going and going."

Reen snickered. "Thanks, Dad. Can I go to bed now?"

"Yes, honey. Give me a hug and away you go to dreamland."

He hugged her hard and put his face close to hers. "You're a very special person, Reen. You can work this out."

She hugged him back. "Good night, Daddy." She turned and left the room.

He felt a lump in his throat. *She always calls me Daddy when she's troubled.* Nate walked back to his desk and picked up the Proverbs card Reen had chosen. *Train up a child in the way he should go; even when he is old he will not depart from it.* He reinserted it in the deck and picked up his phone. He scrolled through his contact list until he came to Kathryn Frasier's number.

Chapter Forty-Eight

THE WATCH SHOP

"Did my dad bribe you to buy me sports stuff?" Reen and Kate walked along Monroe Avenue on the way to the watch shop.

"Of course not, Reen." They stopped at the corner and Kate pushed the button so they could cross the street. She could see why Nate Penterson was concerned about his daughter. Reen was not her usual dynamic, charge-into-battle self. She had been quiet during their trip to the sports store.

"Your father asked if I could help, since I know a little about running. He thinks you could benefit by doing some jogging, and he wants you to have the right equipment." She switched the bag from SportsWorld to her other hand. "You're going to love these shoes we bought. Maybe we'll go to the track today so you can try them out." The light changed and they started across. "Now we'll get a GPS watch to record all the data about your run, and you'll be all set for action."

They stepped up on the sidewalk, turned right, and walked past the little shops that punctuated the college town. T-shirt stands, coffee shops, and bookstores shared space with boutiques and pizza joints. "Here it is," Kate said as they approached a small storefront at the other end of the block.

A large sign above the door was painted in black letters on a beige background. There was an image of a digital watch on the left and an outline of a pair of running shoes on the right with the shop name It's About Time in bold letters. Beneath the name was written "Watches for runners, walkers, and everyone else."

Inside, a lone salesclerk manned the store. His back was turned to them, and he was adjusting the hands of a large clock on the wall behind the main counter as they came in. He jerked around at the sound of the bell.

Kate thought he looked like her imagination's picture of Ichabod Crane. He was tall and skinny, with a long neck and a prominent Adam's apple. His pale face was topped by wispy strands of strawberry blond hair that reminded Kate of the silks on a corncob.

When his eyes landed on Reen, his face transformed into a huge smile accented by large, protruding teeth.

"Welcome to It's About Time!" he almost shouted. "Come in and you can witness me doing something people say is impossible!"

Reen moved closer. "What?"

"I'm going to turn back the hands of time," he said, as if he were announcing a scientific breakthrough. He held his hands up high, wiggled his fingers, and cracked his knuckles. Then he made a great show of turning toward the clock on the wall. He moved his index finger dramatically toward the minute hand on the clock and set it back five minutes. Then he turned back to them with an enormous smile. "Ta-da!"

Reen smiled and looked up at him. "That was funny."

"Funny?" he said in mock surprise. "It wasn't funny. It was magic!" He blew on his fingers and rubbed his hands together. He dropped his voice to a conspiratorial whisper and leaned over the counter. "For my next trick, I'm going to read your mind."

"I don't believe you can read my mind," she said. She had moved right up to the counter.

"We'll see about that." He put his fingers on the sides of his temples and closed his eyes. "Wait. I'm getting a message. Yes. It's coming through to me. It's transmitting closer ... closer." His eyes popped open, and he threw his hands up in the air. "Yes! I have read your mind!"

"What was I thinking?"

"You want to buy a watch." He grinned down at her, his Adam's apple bobbing up and down. "Am I right?"

"Yes," Reen said and laughed out loud.

Kathryn smiled. "Reen's father wants us to pick out a GPS watch for her so she can keep track of data from her running."

"Oh, I see," he said. "He wants to *watch* you!" Then he threw his head back and emitted a high-pitched laugh.

Kate couldn't help laughing. "That's very funny." She noticed Reen's eyes had brightened.

"Step over here," the salesman said. "We have a special counter for young customers." He bounced around the corner to a display case on the side and spread his hands across the top of the glass. "You'll probably find something in here you like." He leaned toward Reen. "Take your *time*," and yuk-yukked.

Reen put her hands on the edge of the counter and looked up at him. "Do you always make jokes about watches and time?"

"Of course! I'm in the perfect job."

Kate pointed to the case. "Why don't you recommend one to us. This will be Reen's first GPS watch, so it doesn't have to have lots of bells and whistles. Just basic speed, time, and so on."

For fifteen minutes, they discussed the various watches. The salesman was knowledgeable and became serious as he took each watch out for them to examine. Reen liked one with a red wristband, so they settled on it. The clerk put the watch in a sales bag and Kate was in the process of paying when the bell over the door rang. A middle-aged gentleman with gray hair and a dark suit walked in and opened a small gate with a key to give him access behind the counter.

"Donald," he said sternly. "Is everything under control?"

Kate saw the salesman's face go pink. His smile disappeared, and he swallowed hard. "Yes, Dad."

The older man walked around the counter and stood facing Kate and Reen. "I hope you had a good shopping experience." He paused and took a deep breath. "Donald can be a little overbearing at times."

"It's been delightful," Kate said. "Your son is knowledgeable and very entertaining."

Reen retrieved the bag from the top of the counter. Her voice was firm. "He's the greatest salesman I ever knew. I wish I could buy everything from him."

The father looked back and forth between the customers and his son. "Umm," he muttered and walked into the back room of the store.

"Thank you," Donald whispered to them as he handed the receipt to Kathryn.

"It's true. I'm going to buy all my watches from you." Reen gave a sharp nod of her head.

Donald regained his playful expression. "Good. Hurry back soon and remember"—he took his wristwatch off and tossed it in the air—"time flies!"

Reen pointed to him. "Good one."

Outside on the sidewalk, Reen pulled the watch box out of the bag. "That was fun." She took the watch out and put it on her wrist. "But it was weird—what he said at the end."

"What was weird?"

"He said 'Time flies.' That's what Mr. Tyme had on his license plate. It's a clue."

Chapter Forty-Nine

SHABBAT DINNER

"It's almost sundown." Mrs. Goldman motioned everyone to the dining room table. "Kathryn, you and Phil sit over to my right. Cece, you and Ben sit to my left."

Mr. Goldman sat at the far end of the table while Mrs. Goldman lit the candles and prayed. "Blessed are you, O Lord our God, King of the universe, who has sanctified us by Your commandments and enjoined upon us the kindling of the sabbath lights."

Mr. Goldman prayed over the red wine, and they all tasted its sweet flavor. Then he prayed over the bread, and they passed the challah loaf around so each person could take a piece.

"Mrs. Goldman, you've made Friday dinner my favorite meal of the week," Ben said.

"That's quite a compliment, Ben. Thank you." Sylvia Goldman glowed as she passed a platter of roast turkey to him. "It seems like we always get a blessing when we have all of you around our table." She reached over to put her hand on Kathryn's arm. "Our very special family."

As they dove into the turkey, sweet potatoes, and asparagus, they each took a turn telling something special that had happened to them during the week. Cece's entry was the rehearsal, with Joanie standing in for another child. "She's really quite good. She's quiet and teachable, and the director thinks he would like her to try out the next time he has a young girl role to cast." She took a bite of turkey. "And her mother enrolled her in a two-week program called Acting Kids. They do all sorts of playacting and even have costumes. I think Joanie is loving it." She sipped her water. "Unfortunately, it's taken her away from her cousin, Reen."

Kate told them about her telephone call from Nate Penterson and the subsequent shopping trip. "Reen was upset because she didn't have Joanie to play with, and he thought I might be able to interest her in running."

"How did it work out?" Ben asked.

Kate chuckled. "The trip to the watch shop was hilarious. The salesman was funny and took a great interest in Reen. By the time we left the shop, she was back to her old self again."

"Hmm," Phil said. "I'm not so sure that's a good thing."

Kathryn elbowed him. "She's really a wonderful girl. It's true she's very assertive for a ten-year-old, but I think that will serve her well in life."

"Was she excited about the watch?" Sylvia asked.

"Oh yes. The salesman made a funny remark about how time flies and threw his watch up in the air. Reen thought that was priceless. Oh, that reminds me." Kathryn put her fork down and took another sip of wine. "Something Reen told me when we left the shop."

"What?" Cece asked.

"She told me she and Joanie had gone to Mr. Tyme's office with Dr. Drafton and they found an old automobile license plate Mr. Tyme had hidden there. It was a vanity plate and it said T-Y-M-F-L-Y-Z."

"Time flies?" Ben asked.

"Right. Reen said it must be a clue. Of course, she thinks everything is a clue, but it is odd that he hid it under his desk. And there was something scratched on the back of it."

"Now that does sound interesting," Mr. Goldman said. "What was it?"

Kate sat forward in her chair. "It was just three letters. K-M-C. I asked Reen how she remembered the letters and she explained a mnemonic Joanie came up with." She grinned. "It's a very unrealistic mnemonic."

"Which is?" Cece asked.

"Kathryn Makes Cookies." Kate laughed. "That's an easy one to remember because I never bake anything."

The others chuckled.

Phil leaned toward the table. "I remember reading a newspaper article once about a man who had murdered his wife, but no one suspected him.

Then he had a vanity license plate made that said 'FREE' and the month and day his wife was killed. Once somebody noticed it, the police got suspicious and found the murder weapon in his house." He looked pensive. "Maybe the license plate is a clue after all."

"But how could it be?" Kate asked. "It's just a vanity license plate. What could it have to do with Mr. Tyme's murder?"

Everyone at the table turned to Phil and waited as he stared into the candlelight in front of him.

Finally, he looked up. "Dr. Malone was injured by a hit-and-run driver, right?"

They all nodded.

"Suppose the clue in the prayer request encoded the license plate number somehow?"

Kathryn gasped. "Of course. It fits. Mr. Tyme must have made the connection between the prayer request and the license plate of the car that injured Dr. Malone. That's what he was going to meet someone about the night he died." She jumped up, ran to get her purse, and pulled the slip of paper out. "The proverb at the top refers to a king."

Phil took the paper from her. "Then it says 'Keep My Commandments 728.' He looked at Kate and smiled. "Keep My Commandments. Kathryn Makes Cookies. K-M-C. It's a code for license plate number KMC728."

There were gasps all around the table. "Of course," Cece said.

Kate gave Phil a big kiss. "You're a genius."

He grinned. "Maybe I should work with you more often."

Chapter Fifty

THE LICENSE PLATE

MacMillan clicked his phone off and turned to his partner. "That was Kathryn Frasier. She wanted to know what we found out about the license plate."

Carlioni gulped down the last bit of coffee and shook his head. "What license plate?"

"She said some professor found a license plate that belonged to Mr. Tyme and he thinks it's a clue to Mr. Tyme's murder."

"She knows we're not working that case." Carlioni put his head in his hands and moaned. "What did I ever do to deserve this?"

MacMillan got a thoughtful look on his face. "Kathryn says she thinks it could also be a clue in Dr. Malone's hit-and-run accident."

Now Carlioni lifted his head and looked at his partner. "Where is this license plate?"

"She says this professor guy gave it to Officer Olssen, who supposedly was going to look into it. I'm guessing he reported it to our super-duper interim commissioner."

"Nobody told me about it." Carlioni stood. "We need to check this out."

There was a knock at the door. "Come in," Carlioni shouted.

Kathryn opened the door and peered in. "Got a minute?"

"Always have time for you," MacMillan said and pulled a chair around for her to sit.

"Tell us about this license plate." Carlioni picked up a stress ball from his desk and squeezed it.

"I don't know if this is a clue, but I have a feeling," Kathryn said.

Carlioni pursed his lips and squeezed the ball tighter. "Feelings don't solve crimes, Miss Frasier. We're interested in the facts."

"Exactly." Kathryn sat and leaned forward.

"Tell us everything you know," MacMillan said.

"One of the professors was in Mr. Tyme's office along with the little girls."

"Oh no. Don't tell me the children found the clue to solve a murder!" Carlioni harrumphed and tossed the stress ball up in the air.

"Wait a second, Carli," his partner said. "Stranger things have happened. Let's hear what she has to say."

"They found the license plate stuck under the slats on the bottom of Mr. Tyme's desk."

"I admit that's pretty strange," Carlioni said. "Go on."

"We know Mr. Tyme was going to meet with someone. Maybe it's possible he left the license plate as a clue just in case the real killer got on to him."

"So, what's so special about this license plate?" Carlioni asked.

"It's a vanity plate. It's spelled T-Y-M-F-L-Y-Z. You know, like 'time flies.'"

"Lots of people have vanity plates. Doesn't make them crime solvers."

"Yes, but this one had the letters K-M-C scratched on the back. We think it could be a clue to Dr. Malone's hit-and-run."

"I'm listening." Carlioni put the stress ball back on his desk.

"Remember, there were two clues before Mr. Tyme died. The first one had to do with Dr. Silva and the second one we think was Dr. Malone. Suppose Mr. Tyme had an idea about how to decode the second one? Maybe he met with someone to explain that he decoded the king clue, and he knew how to find the person who tried to kill Dr. Malone."

Carlioni picked up the copy of the king clue that had been lying on his desk. "This one? You think this has something to do with a license plate?"

Kathryn nodded. "See, the proverb at the top is about the king. The second line says 'Keep My Commandments 728.'" Then it says 'God Remembers' at the bottom."

"I don't get it," MacMillan said. "What does this have to do with a license plate?"

Kate pointed to the middle line. "Keep My Commandments 728 may be the license plate number."

"Kinda long for a license plate, isn't it?" Carlioni snorted.

"It's a mnemonic."

"A what?" Carlioni wrinkled his brow.

"A mnemonic. It's a way to remember things. Whoever's leaving these clues is very clever. We know they like to encode things, so the mnemonic could be the way to remember the license plate." Kate leaned against the desk. "Keep My Commandments 728 could just be a code for 'KMC 728.' That could be a license plate."

MacMillan and Carlioni exchanged a look. MacMillan took the slip of paper from Carlioni. "It makes sense, Carli."

"Hmm." Carlioni held his hand out and took the paper back from MacMillan. "You could be right." He studied the paper. "Mac, it's time for us to pay a visit to Samantha Simpkins."

* * *

Carlioni and MacMillan approached the Office of the Interim Police Commissioner as a balding, round, bearded man come out. Samantha Simpkins accompanied him. "Mr. Clayborne, you are the most perceptive man I've ever met." She put her hand on his arm. "The mayor is so lucky to have you."

The man grinned. His florid face turned even redder, and he lifted his chin. "Thank you, Samantha, and you are one of a kind. You're the best commissioner this town has ever had. The way you've handled all these cases shows me we selected the right person to take over this interim position. The mayor wants to talk to you about next steps in your career soon."

Carlioni cleared his throat. "Ms. Simpkins, we need to talk to you about new evidence—"

"Not now." She held up a polished index finger in front of Carlioni, then turned back to Mr. Clayborne. "Please give the mayor my regards and tell him I'll be happy to meet with him at his convenience."

Carlioni stepped in front of her. "We have new evidence in the Malone hit-and-run case. We need to discuss the investigation with you."

Simpkins glared at him. "Talk to Lonnie. You can set up an appointment this afternoon."

"The Malone case?" Mr. Clayborne looked at Simpkins. "The mayor is very concerned about the Malone case. Dr. Malone is making a lot of noise about it, and we've been getting bad press lately." He removed her hand from his arm and turned to Carlioni. "I'm Conrad Clayborne, the mayor's chief of staff, and I'd like to hear what you have to say."

They shook hands. "Nice to meet you, Mr. Clayborne. I'm Detective Carlioni, and this is my partner, Detective MacMillan. We've received information that may bear on the Malone case. It has to do with a license plate."

"Oh, that," Simpkins said.

"What license plate?" Clayborne asked.

Simpkins fiddled with the earring in her left ear. "Some kids found a license plate in Mr. Tyme's office and decided it had something to do with his death. You know kids. They jumped to a conclusion based on practically nothing. And it doesn't have anything to do with Dr. Malone."

"We think it has a direct bearing on the Malone case." Carlioni's mouth hardened into a straight line.

"I'd like to hear more about this," Clayborne said and motioned to Carlioni. "Let's go back into Ms. Simpkins's office and you can fill me in."

Chapter Fifty-One

JOANIE

Joanie said goodbye to Abigail Leister, the beautiful grad student who was directing the Acting Kids summer program. Joanie had determined to be just like her when she grew up.

Abigail stooped down. "Joanie, you did such a great job today as the little urchin. And you look so cute in these overalls." She touched the shoulder strap of the denim outfit. "It's the perfect costume for your role."

"It's funny," Joanie said. "This is just like the clothes my cousin Reen wears. I'm going to tell her she's a little urchin."

"Ha. That's great. Tell Reen we'd like her to come to Acting Kids too. Oh, and by the way, tell your mom there was a mix-up, and another kid took your regular clothes home with them. We'll straighten it out next time. In the meantime, you can wear the overalls."

"Thanks, Abigail. Goodbye." Joanie waved.

"Goodbye. It's getting late so be careful going home."

Joanie headed out across the quad. It was quiet now. The clouds were moving in, and everyone seemed to have left campus.

She saw the man as she turned the corner next to the library. He was sitting on the bench next to the bell tower, and at first she thought it must be Mr. Venero because he was wearing a big, floppy hat. But when she got closer, she realized it couldn't be Mr. Venero. The man on the bench was larger than the gardener.

My father! Of course! He must have come to campus to find her after the scene they had last night when her parents had argued and she had begged him to take her away with him. She told him how sad she was, but he said he couldn't take her, and she had cried and run to her room. He must have felt bad and now he was here.

She skipped over to him, and he looked up.

It wasn't her father but another man. He had a handsome smile and his face looked kind.

"Well, hello," he said. "You must be the Penterson girl. I've been waiting for you."

Joanie nodded. Everybody thought her last name was Penterson because she had red hair and because her mother had kept her maiden name when she married.

"I'm so glad you came this way," he said. "Your father wanted me to take you to him."

"My father?" Joanie felt her heart leap. Her mother had told her never to talk to strangers, but this man knew her father.

"He said he wants to talk to you about the clue you found. You know, about that murder." The man looked intently at her. "He said you know the license plate of a car and he wants me to take you to him so you can both go to the police."

Joanie realized he must be talking about the license plate she and Reen had found under the desk in Mr. Tyme's office. "That's right," she said. "I found the license plate."

"Great." The man stood. He was tall and looked very kind. "Let's go to your dad." He held out his hand, and she took it. It was warm and large. They began to walk toward the bell tower door. "Here," he said, and handed her a big sugar cookie. "Your dad wanted you to have this. He said you'd be hungry."

Chapter Fifty-Two

CECE GETS IT

Cece ambled down the side aisle in the dark theater and climbed the stairs. She walked to center stage and stood facing the empty house. Then she made a sweeping curtsy in response to imaginary applause.

This was her space. The silence of the massive room was a comfort, and she felt her skin tingle at the thought of standing before a real audience in a couple of weeks. It was so dark she could barely make out the orchestra pit in front of the stage, but she knew exactly where it was. She turned and moved the flowing velvet curtain to one side.

A dim light illuminated the backstage area, and she pushed open the door to the wardrobe room. It smelled musty, with a cocktail of perfumes that actors had used over the years. Plumed hats and bright costumes brought out a smile, and she strolled beside the row of costumes, letting her hand brush over the silks and satins that had adorned the stage in years past.

Although the theater was locked, Alan had loaned her the key to the front door, and she loved being alone in the building. It reminded her of happy afternoons in her parents' home playing dress-up in the attic and acting out all the parts in her own plays. When she reached the end of the clothes rack, she smiled at the large rubber snake that had frightened Joanie.

All she had intended to do was return the costume, wig, and earrings she had used as Rose Ramen. She placed the hairpiece on one of the mannequin heads and went to the corner where shelves of hats were stored. She took her phone out of her pocket and hit the Record button. *May as well practice a little dialect while I'm here.*

She laid her phone on the shelf, took down a large straw bonnet, and tried it on. She posed in front of the mirror and intoned in a heavy southern accent, "Why, Daisy Mae, you're just as pretty as a picture."

She replaced the hat, took down a tiara, and placed it on her head. Then she stood with her nose pointed up and held an imaginary sword. "I dub thee Sir Benjamin," she announced. *I really should bring Ben here.*

She took the tiara off and moved the headpieces around to make room for it on the shelf. Her hand bumped a crown that rolled off and fell on the floor. She picked it up. "Apologies, sire," she said. "It isn't meet to knock the king's hat off." She lowered her voice to a deep, hoarse tone. "Clumsy girl. I'll have your head. Page, take this silly woman to the courtyard. I'll send for the regiment to form a firing squad." She giggled at her own silliness. "The regiment, sire?" She sat on a trunk and held the crown in her hands.

"I guess regiment comes from the root of the Latin word for 'king.' I'll have to tell Reggie his name actually means King." She held the crown up. "I dub thee King Reggie." Then she clapped her hand over her mouth and felt her eyes open wide. "Reggie," she whispered. "Reggie. The king."

She stood and screwed her face into a ball of concentration. She stared at the crown she was holding. "Names have meanings," she said aloud.

She put the crown back on the shelf and noticed the Star of David, a prop that had been used in a previous play and was hanging on the wall along with other religious symbols. She stared at it. A thought bubbled up from her subconscious. "Mel," she said. "Melech is Hebrew for 'king.' I should tell Kathryn. Maybe Mel Silva's first name is actually Melech." She thought she heard a noise out in the theater, and she stopped to listen, but there was only silence.

She took the Rose Ramen costume out of the canvas bag and hung the various parts on empty coat hangers. Then she walked behind the racks of clothes to the other end of the room where the boxes of fake jewelry were kept. As she pulled the pair of massive earrings out of her pocket, one of them caught on the fabric of her jacket and broke. A shower of little red and gold balls fell to the floor.

Rats. She dropped to her knees and felt around the floor for the tiny ornaments. *Now I'll have to take all the pieces home and put the earrings back together again.* As she groped in the dark room, she heard the door open, and a man's voice invaded the silence. She started to stand up to make her presence known when she heard the words, "Don't worry. I took care of Tyme, and nobody will ever know you drove the car that hit Malone."

Cece felt her heart go into hyper-rhythm. *He must be talking on his phone.* The voice was familiar, but she couldn't place it. She held her breath and crouched behind the rack of costumes.

The voice continued. "I'm putting the phone on speaker so I can change back to my clothes. No problem. I'm in the wardrobe room of the theater. The building's locked and there's nobody else here. I used some old clothes from the theater to look like Venero, just in case anybody saw me take the Penterson girl."

Take the Penterson girl? Take her where? Cece felt her heart freeze. She eased a shawl aside that was hanging on the rack and peeked into the dark room. The man's back was turned to her, but she saw him put an object on the shelf next to the wall. It looked like a gun.

A woman's voice came through his phone. "I am worried. Venero saw me that night. Even though I was wearing the redhead wig, he knew me. He actually called me by my name when he tapped on the car window and asked if I was all right. I yelled at him to go away."

"We've been over all of this before. Venero's a simpleton. Even if he could remember, nobody would believe him. I'm more worried about the Penterson girl. She found a license plate that might give the police enough information to discover it was the car we rented in California." Cece's breath caught in her throat, and she clenched her fists tight to keep from making any noise.

The man continued. "But she's out of the picture now. Her life is literally in God's hands, and at eight o'clock she won't be a danger to us anymore. I left a note in the chapel prayer box signed by Venero admitting to the murder of the girl."

Cece couldn't control the electric jolt that shot through her body. She jumped up and faced the man. Her hand shook as she pointed to him and screamed, "You! What have you done?"

Mel Silva wheeled around and his eyes bulged out in shock. He was wearing a khaki jacket and a pair of pants that resembled Mr. Venero's usual outfit. A floppy hat lay on the floor by his feet. "W-What are you doing here?"

"Mel. Mel, what's happening?" The woman's voice came through his phone, and he punched it off.

"What did you hear?" he demanded and moved toward Cece.

"Enough," she said. She hardly recognized her own voice. She turned toward the door.

Silva took two quick steps and grabbed her arm. His face was contorted in savage fury, and his breath was loud and ragged. Cece pulled hard, but he held fast. "You're not going anywhere," he said. "I have a gun." He started to drag her back to the shelf where he had laid his firearm.

Cece felt a surge of adrenaline through every cell in her body. "Snake!" she screamed and pointed beyond him. When he turned, he loosened his grip just enough, and she jerked free. She leaped for the door, ran out, and slammed it behind her.

Chapter Fifty-Three

WAITING FOR CECE

Kathryn and Phil sat on the bench under the oak tree. "How long does it take her to return one wig and a costume to the theater?" he asked.

Kate laughed. "Cece? She may try on all the costumes in the wardrobe room before she comes out. You'd better relax. It may be a while."

"Hey, Kathryn," a voice called from the far side of the quad. Reen jogged over to them.

"Well, hello there, fellow runner." Kate pointed at the girl's shoes. "Looks like you're putting some miles on those shoes."

"Yep. My dad says I can't do any more investigating until I run ten miles."

"How many have you done?" Phil asked.

"A little over five, but it took me a couple of days to do that."

"So you're running this evening to build up some more miles?" Kate asked.

"No. I'm looking for Joanie. Her mother called and said she didn't come home from acting class, and she wanted to know if she was at my house." She shrugged. "Her mother's the worrying type, you know."

"It's nice of you to look for her."

Reen pushed her bottom lip out. "I told Mrs. Toussaint I shouldn't have to look for Joanie. If she's big enough to go to acting class alone, she's big enough to find her own way home."

Kate raised her eyebrows. "What did Mrs. Toussaint say?"

"She told me to stop being a fusspot and go find her." Reen sighed. "Mrs. Toussaint always takes Joanie's side."

"Did you try the Acting Kids program in the drama building?" Kate asked.

"I went there, but they said she left an hour ago. I thought she might be at the theater, but the door's locked, so I'm going to try the playground. She sometimes stops there on her way home."

"Good idea. You check the playground. We'll call Cece and have her let us in the theater."

"Thanks, Kathryn. Call me if you find Joanie." She jogged off in the direction of the playground.

"What was all that about?" Phil asked.

Kate grimaced. "Reen and Joanie had a little spat because Joanie wanted to do some acting instead of assisting Reen with her murder investigation. I guess Reen still has some bad feelings about it."

* * *

Kate pulled her phone out, punched an icon, and waited. "Cece's not answering her phone."

"That's not surprising," Phil said. "She's probably acting out all the roles of *Macbeth* on stage with her phone turned off. Let's go knock on the door. Maybe she'll hear us."

As they walked toward the theater, there was a sound of tires screeching in the parking lot next to the quad. "It's the detectives," Kate said. They changed course and jogged over to the lot.

Carlioni had stopped the car behind a light blue Lexus in the parking lot. MacMillan jumped out of the passenger side and checked the license plate of the other car.

"This is it," he said to Carlioni, who had cut the ignition and stepped out on the driver's side.

"What's up?" Phil asked.

"This is Mel Silva's car," Carlioni answered. "Have you seen him?"

"No," Kate said. "Why are you looking for him?"

"We got some info on that license plate idea of yours. Look at this." He took a sheet of yellow lined paper out of his pocket and unfolded it. "Here are all the states with 6-digit license plates. We checked each of these for a plate that matched KMC 728."

Kate wanted to hug him. "And?"

"We found that number in several states, but one really jumped out."

"Way to go, guys." Phil shook his head in admiration. "You may have solved the case."

Carlioni's face turned grim. "It was a rental car with a Montana license plate. We contacted the company and found out the car had been rented at the Oakland, California airport two days before Malone's accident and was returned to the same place five days later. The person who rented it paid cash."

"So we don't know who rented it?" Kate's smile faded.

"No, but we know something even better," MacMillan said. "The rental car company is responsible for getting the driver's license. That driver's license in their files belongs to Janelle Kaiser."

"Janelle Kaiser drove the car that hit Dr. Malone? Why would she do that?" Phil asked.

"We don't have all the answers, but we figured the car was damaged after she hit Malone, so we checked car repair companies in all the states in the area and found one in Nevada that had repaired the front right fender on that car the day after Malone's accident. The bill was paid with a credit card. Care to guess whose it was?"

"You better tell us," Kate said.

"Mel Silva's." Carlioni grunted in disgust.

"Silva?" Kate said. "But Silva was one of the people who was targeted. How could it be him?"

MacMillan ran a hand through his hair. "We don't know, but we're guessing Silva was furious because Malone cost him his job and his wife's money, so he talked Janelle into driving the car that was intended to kill Malone."

"Revenge is a powerful motivator," Carlioni said.

"So you think Dr. Silva is somewhere on campus now?" Phil asked.

"Looks that way. We put an APB out. One of our guys spotted his car here."

* * *

Cece stood completely still between the curtains and tried to quiet her breathing. It had taken Silva a few seconds to get his gun, and that had given her an advantage. Even in the pitch black, she knew the backstage of the theater like the back of her own hand. She crept along between the curtains. When she got to the other side of the stage, she could hear him fumbling. *He must be looking for the lights. If he finds them, I'm dead.*

"Cece. Cece, where are you? Let's talk this out. I can explain everything." Silva's voice had a smooth, oily tone to it.

Yeah, right. I bet we're just going to be best buds from now on.

She eased her way along the wings. There was a prop table at the edge of the stage. She gingerly reached over to pick up a small clock on the edge of the table, but she misjudged the distance and the clock teetered and fell off the edge. She grabbed it before it hit the floor and slung it toward the first row of seats, where it made a loud thump. A shot rang out.

Cece's heart beat so hard she thought Silva must be able to hear it. She heard his steps as he crossed the stage toward her. *He must be right at the footlights. If he gets much closer, he'll spot me.* She carefully picked up a metronome from the table, quietly unhooked the arm, and held it from swinging. She stood for a second, gauging the distance. Then she took a quiet breath and tossed the device. It dropped into the orchestra pit and made a clattering crash when it hit one of the music stands, and the metronome arm continued to click back and forth. There were two more shots, then another loud crash. Silva yelled a string of obscenities. Cece jumped down from the stage into the side aisle and raced toward the front door of the theater.

Chapter Fifty-Four

THE MIXUP

Kate's head jerked up when the front door of the theater building flew open and she heard Cece shout, "Kathryn! Phil! Help!" Cece raced toward them, her hands waving wildly.

"It's Silva!" Cece screamed as she got closer. "He was in the theater. I got away from him and I think he fell into the orchestra pit." She gulped a huge breath. "He's got a gun."

"Get back." Carlioni pointed behind them. "Take cover behind that bench."

He and MacMillan pulled their Glock-19s and started toward the theater.

The door to the theater banged open and Mel Silva stood framed in the doorway with a gun in his hand. He hobbled forward a few steps.

"Drop your gun!" Carlioni shouted.

Silva turned to his right and ran along the front of the building toward the parking lot, favoring his left leg as he went.

A dapper figure appeared at the corner of the building. Dr. Drafton!

"Get down!" Carlioni screamed at Drafton. "He has a gun."

Dr. Drafton froze, staring at the man limping toward him.

"Get away," Silva shouted and waved his gun at Drafton.

Drafton stepped aside. As Silva limped by, Dr. Drafton cocked his walking stick back like a major league baseball bat and swung viciously at Silva's injured leg.

Silva screamed and lurched forward, crashing to the ground. His gun skidded across the grass. As Silva lay writhing in pain, Drafton picked the gun up and pointed it at him. The detectives ran up. While MacMillan carefully removed the gun from Dr. Drafton's grip, Carlioni pulled Silva's hands behind his back and cuffed him.

Cece grabbed Kate by the shoulders. "He's going to kill Reen! He set something up." Cece gasped for air. "He said, 'The Penterson girl's life is in God's hands.' He said she would die at eight o'clock."

"Me?" Reen's voice came out of nowhere. She jogged up from behind.

Cece let go of Kate and ran to the young girl. "Reen! You're all right." She hugged the child so tight Reen said "Ouch."

"He said he was going to hurt the Penterson girl?" Kate swung around to look at Reen. "Did you find Joanie in the playground?"

"No." Reen looked up at her. "She wasn't in the theater?"

Kate felt a cold knot in the center of her chest. "He wasn't talking about Reen. He must have gotten her mixed up with Joanie."

"What could it mean?" Cece asked. "Her life is in God's hands. It must be some kind of code."

"Whatever it is, we don't have much time." Phil looked at his watch. "It's five minutes to eight now."

Kate raised her eyes and looked toward the bell tower. "Her life is in God's hands." She stared at the clock embedded in the rough-hewn stone. "It's the bell tower. He's got her in the bell tower."

"Oh, no!" Reen screamed. "Joanie!" She raced toward the tower with Phil, Kate, and Cece right behind.

Chapter Fifty-Five

FOR WHOM THE BELL TOLLS

Phil got to the bell tower first and pulled on the door, but it wouldn't budge. He yanked hard, but it stayed fast. He turned to Kate. "It's locked. See if you can find a key."

"Help her!" Reen screamed.

Zack Venero appeared from the side of the bell tower, obviously alarmed at the noise. "What's going on here?" he demanded.

Kathryn grabbed his arm. "We need your key to the bell tower. Joanie may be inside. She's in danger."

Venero's eyes bulged. "I don't have my keys," he said. "I left them in the cottage when I heard the noise."

Kathryn's hands flew to her face. "Oh, no. We have to get to her."

"Wait." He turned and disappeared around the side of the tower.

Kate looked up and saw Reen climbing up the rugged stone facade. Kathryn gasped, afraid to say anything that might cause the girl to fall. As she watched, Reen got to the clock face and grabbed onto the hour hand that was just moving toward the eight. Kate started up the wall. The stones were uneven, but her hands and feet were too big to get a good hold. She only got a few feet off the ground when she slipped and fell back.

Mr. Venero came back, holding a ladder. "Maybe I can reach her with this."

Kate pointed to Reen. "She's going to try to stop the hands from moving."

Venero propped the ladder against the side of the tower. It wasn't tall enough to reach the clock face, but it was close. "I'll go," Kathryn said.

"No." Venero blocked her way. He pulled his shoes off and started up. When he reached the top of the ladder, he still had several yards to go before he could grasp the hands of the clock. Reen was hanging on the hour hand. Kathryn held her breath as Venero pulled himself up.

She looked at her watch. 7:57. Three minutes to go. She heard the loud click as the tower clock's minute hand moved. Two minutes to go.

Dr. Drafton shuffled up as fast as he could, huffing with his effort across the quad. "Here. I have a master key." He handed the keyring to Phil with the large gold key protruding. The click sounded again. One minute to go.

Kathryn watched as Venero reached up, grabbed the hour hand and braced himself. She could hear his voice clearly as he directed Reen. "Put your hands on the hour hand like I have and pull carefully. We won't let it progress, but we have to be sure not to break it." Kate saw him help Reen into position. The young girl was wedged between Venero and the wall of the tower. They were both holding on to the hour hand.

Phil unlocked the door and yanked it open. He and Cece disappeared inside the tower, and Kathryn raced up the stairs behind them.

* * *

Holding onto the hour hand, Zachary Venero felt his hands burning, and he knew Reen's hands must be scorched by the iron that had been heated in the afternoon sun. "Are you all right?" he asked. He took a chance and let his right hand drop to pull a handkerchief out of his pocket. "Put this under your hands." He maneuvered the cloth onto the hour hand.

The child said nothing but put her hands on top of the handkerchief.

"Now hold tight," Venero said. "We want to keep the gears from turning, but we can't pull too hard or we'll break the hand off."

Reen was sobbing. "Please save her."

"Brace yourself against the bricks like I am." His voice was soft, but firm. "Don't worry. She'll be all right."

They held fast. The last click had taken them to within one minute of the clock chiming. If only the others would hurry.

Zachary could feel the hour hand struggling to move forward. "Have faith," he said. "We can do this."

Click.

Chapter Fifty-Six

REEN IN THE HOSPITAL

A real reporter showed up at the hospital this morning to interview me. Dad shooed him away and said he could come back when I was feeling better. I'm feeling great, though. All except my hands. They got burned by the clock.

Dr. Silva had given Joanie some kind of sleeping thing, so she never knew she was in any danger. My dad said they kept her in the hospital overnight just to watch her.

Mr. Venero was real strong, and he kept me from slipping while we held onto the hour hand. We heard Phil shout, "We have her!" when they got to Joanie and carried her out of the bell tower. Then Mr. Venero told them to get the long ladder out of his tool shed and he held me while we climbed down. He's my hero. Next to my dad, of course.

The doctors made me stay overnight, so I slept in a hospital bed with big bandages around both hands. Dad stayed with me, and this morning he gave me a chocolate milkshake.

Kathryn and Phil were the first ones to come to the room. She had a bandage on her hand where she sprained it when she fell off the bell tower. She said we were two of a kind, and we held our hands up together so Phil could take a picture.

Then Cece and her boyfriend, Ben, came in. Ben is a cool guy. He wears a cowboy hat and boots, and he owns a ranch with horses. He said I could come ride his horses anytime I want to. I can't wait.

Mrs. Toussaint and Miss Culberson showed up at the same time, and they looked like they were having a competition to see who could get through the door first. Mrs. Toussaint won, of course. She brought me a container of brownies and looked at me like I was some kind of angel. Then she turned to Miss Culberson and said, "Reen is so athletic. All that tree-climbing made her strong enough to climb up the side of the bell tower!" I hope that means we can skip the pimento cheese sandwiches for a while.

Miss Culberson retorted, "It's the books she reads. She's always thinking and trying to figure things out. She has a brilliant mind." She patted me on the arm and gave me a book about how the Nancy Drew mysteries were written.

Dr. Drafton came in and told everybody Joanie and I were the smartest children he ever knew. Then he went and stood next to Miss Culberson, and he even put his arm around her.

Dad grinned so wide, I thought he might damage his face.

Everybody got real respectful when Reverend and Mrs. Whitefield came in along with Cece's parents. There was also a rabbi and his wife. Mrs. Toussaint and Miss Culberson were kind of bowing and they looked like they were being introduced to the heavenly host. Mrs. Whitefield brought a plate of something she called blueberry scones, and it turned into a party.

Detectives Carlioni and MacMillan showed up, and Mac said he wanted me to be a part of their team when I grow up. Carlioni said he was going to take up rock climbing.

Donald from the watch shop came in and gave me a miniature version of the bell tower. "You really did it," he said. "You turned back the hands of time."

Everybody was laughing and having a good time when Joanie walked in with her parents. She was holding her father's hand. She came over and put her hand on my arm and wanted to know if I was okay. I said yes, and Aunt Melissa started to cry. Then Uncle Jayce leaned over and whispered in my ear. He said he never knew how much he loved his family until today, and he thanked me too. You should have seen Joanie's face. She looked like a Christmas tree all lit up.

She asked me if she could still be my assistant, and I said "No." The lights in her face dimmed when I said that, but I did it on purpose just so I could spring my surprise on her. I said, "I want you to be my partner in my new venture." That cranked the lights up even higher.

"What will we do?" she asked.

"I'm going to write murder mysteries. You can be my agent."

Joanie jumped up and down and clapped her hands. It was just like old times. When she came back down to earth, she asked, "What does an agent do?"

"The agent tells a publisher how wonderful the stories are, so the publisher will publish the books," I said. "Agents are really good at make-believe, so you'll be a natural."

Everybody laughed and talked some more and then Mr. Venero came in.

He was carrying a little flower. He called it an impatiens, and I told him it was a pretty good plant for me. He seemed to like that. Dad asked him to sit down, and they talked for a long time about plants. Mr. Venero knows everything. When he got up to go, he took something out of his pocket. "This is for Reen," he said. It was his pocket watch.

Dad said, "That's too expensive, Zack. She can't accept it."

Mr. Venero's eyes looked a little teary, and he faced my dad. "My best friend gave me this watch just before he died. He told me, 'God wants us to remember to use our time on earth for good.'" He handed it to me. "I want Reen to have it."

Dad said it was okay, and Mr. Venero patted my shoulder and then he left. I opened the watch and there was an inscription inside. Kathryn wanted to know what was written there. It said *Our lives are in God's hands.*

Everybody started to cry. Even Mrs. Toussaint.

Chapter Fifty-Seven

THE CODE

Kathryn left the hospital with Phil and some of the others, including Cece and Ben, Cece's parents, Reverend and Mrs. Whitefield, Rabbi and Mrs. Hart, and the detectives. As they walked toward the quad, Reverend Whitefield turned to Phil and asked, "What happened in the bell tower when you finally got in last evening?"

Phil stopped, and the others gathered around. "Joanie was asleep in the corner of the tower. Apparently, Silva had drugged her. She never knew anything."

"I thought you said he was going to kill her," Rabbi Hart said.

"That's right," Cece said. "When we got up to the bell room, we discovered what he meant." She nodded toward Phil. "Phil understood it right away."

Phil pointed toward the tower. "Silva had rigged up a mechanism to blow up the bell tower and Joanie along with it."

"No!" Jan Whitefield gasped and put her hand to her heart.

Phil's expression turned grim. "He had set a container of fuel oil on top of a crate. When the hammer arm swung out, it would have hit the container and made the fuel drop into a canister of explosive. If it had gone off, it would have been a disaster."

"When we got up there, Phil moved the table with the fuel oil out of the way," Kathryn said. "While Cece and I were trying to get Joanie up, he also moved the other canister to the side and called the fire department. By the time we all got downstairs and Mr. Venero got Reen down off the clock, the gears turned and the hammer struck the bell eight times. No one probably noticed the clock was a few minutes late striking on the hour."

"Right," Phil said. "The fire department first responders arrived in just a few minutes and took all the explosive material away."

"Thank God," Reverend Whitefield said.

Kate turned to Detective Carlioni. "What will happen to Dr. Silva and Janelle Kaiser? Is there enough evidence to convict them?"

Carlioni nodded. "Thanks to Cece, we have Silva's and Kaiser's complete confessions." He pointed his pencil at Cece. "Her phone was recording the entire time Silva talked to Janelle about the attempted murder of Dr. Malone and the real murder of Mr. Tyme. They won't be seeing the outside of a prison for a long time."

"You see," Ben said as he put his arm around Cece. "I knew you were a great detective. You got the confession of not just one criminal, but two."

"Ha!" Cece looked up at him and smirked. "I can't imagine anyone less likely to get a confession than me. But there's something that still confuses me."

They all turned to her.

"This whole thing started with a prayer request and a code. The murder was solved, but we never deciphered the code."

"That's right," Kate said. "And we still don't know who put the prayer requests in the prayer box."

Mr. Goldman chuckled. "Knowing you two, you'll figure it out somehow." He turned to Reverend Whitefield. "It was touching what Mr. Venero said about how God wants us to remember to use our time on earth for good."

Reverend Whitefield's face grew soft. "Zachary was deeply affected by his friend's death."

"Zachary?" Rabbi Hart tilted his head to the side. "Mr. Venero's first name is Zachary?"

"Yes," Kate said. "Why?"

"In Hebrew, the name Zachary means 'God Remembers.'"

Kate slapped the palm of her hand to her forehead. "Of course!" she said. "It was Mr. Venero who put the prayer requests in the box. He didn't do it to turn in a murderer. He did it because he was offering prayers for people he thought needed them."

"I get it," Cece said. "The clue 'Remove the dross from the silver' just meant that Dr. Silva needed purification from his sin. Remember, Dr. Malone said everybody knew what was going on, even Mr. Venero."

"Right," Kate said. "What about the king clue?"

Cece held her phone up. "Janelle said she yelled at Mr. Venero in the parking lot. That must have been the reference to the growling king. Her name Kaiser means emperor in German. Mr. Venero encoded the license plate of the car she was driving."

"And the coal clue documented Mr. Tyme's death." Kate sighed. "Mr. Venero was sincerely praying for the soul of a friend."

"But we never figured out the code," Cece said.

They walked on until they reached the bench under the same oak tree that Reen had fallen out of. Kate looked back at the hospital. "I think I know how to decipher the code now." She sat down on the bench and took a notebook out of her purse. "Dr. Cassidy told me it's possible to encode a message by using another message as the key."

She turned the page to a blank sheet. "I believe the key to the code is what was written inside Mr. Venero's pocket watch—'Our lives are in God's hands.'"

"That makes sense," Reverend Whitefield said. "Can you decode it now?"

Kate wrote the letters of the alphabet down and mapped the key to it. "If the key has any letters that are repeated, you have to skip them."

```
ABCDEFGHIJKLMNOPQRSTUVWXYZ
ourlivesangdh
```

"But then you have letters of the alphabet left over," Phil said.

"Right. So you just add whatever letters in the regular alphabet that haven't been used." She finished the key. "Here's what it looks like."

A	B	C	D	E	F	G	H	I	J	K	L	M	N	O	P	Q	R	S	T	U	V	W	X	Y	Z
o	u	r	l	i	v	e	s	a	n	g	d	h	b	c	f	j	k	m	p	q	t	w	x	y	z

"Then all you have to do is reverse the mapping on the code." She wrote the coded message in large letters so everyone could see.

WAPSPAHIODDPSABEMOKIKITIODIL

"Find the coded letter in the lower-case key and substitute the letter from the alphabet."

"I see," MacMillan said. "The coded letter *w* maps to *W*, and the next letter *a* maps to *I*."

"Right," Kate said. "The next coded letter is *p*."

"That maps to the letter *T*," Carlioni said.

"And the next letter *s* maps to *H*," Ben said.

Mr. Goldman nodded his understanding. "So the first word is *WITH*."

"And the next four letters map to *TIME*," Phil said.

Kathryn looked up at Phil and touched his hand. "I think I see where this is going."

"I see it," Rabbi Hart said. "The next three letters spell *ALL*."

Reverend and Mrs. Whitefield worked the next letters together. "The next word looks like *THING*," Jan said.

Reverend Whitefield noted, "Check the next letter. The word must be *THINGS*."

Sylvia Goldman put her arm around her husband's waist. "I know this saying. The next word is *ARE*."

Kate pointed to each of the last eight letters, one at a time, and the group called out each decoded letter.

As Kate wrote the letters, Mr. Venero appeared at the side of the bell tower, pushing a wheelbarrow of topsoil toward the rectory. He had changed back into his work clothes, and he stopped to remove his hat and